Socialisation and Education

By

V.K. Nanda

ANMOL PUBLICATIONS PVT. LTD.
NEW DELHI - 110 002 (INDIA)

ANMOL PUBLICATIONS PVT. LTD.
H.O.: 4374/4B, Ansari Road, Darya Ganj,
New Delhi-110 002 (India)
Ph.: 23278000, 23261597
B.O.: No. 1015, Ist Main Road, BSK IIIrd Stage
IIIrd Phase, IIIrd Block
Bangalore - 560 085 (India)
Visit us at: www.anmolpublications.com

Socialisation and Education

Reprint, 2008

PRINTED IN INDIA

Printed at Mehra Offset Press, Delhi.

SOCIALISATION AND EDUCATION

Contents

Preface

Socialisation process is in fact is 'education' in itself. In the formal sense education and socialisation are complementary to each other.

The present volume is highly informative and useful for the students, researchers, policy planners and educational administrators.

VKN

1

Formal Doctrine: Manifestations, Content, Dimensions and Consequences

Sometimes a picture of social reality becomes clearer by stepping back from the concrete images of day-to-day activities and events and by viewing the larger context into which the particulars fit. One part of this frame of reference is that we have called the "formal doctrine." Our analysis proceeds this way. All groups and organizations, in the course of their development, build a point of view or perspective about themselves, their problems, and their environment. These points of view vary in the degree to which they are visionary, conscious, and codified. We have come to use the term "formal doctrine" to represent the complex combination of a point of view that is visionary, that is highly conscious, and that is highly codified. Ideology, a visionary theorizing, could serve about as well, although it tends not to emphasize the conscious and codified aspects. The doctrine includes an elaborated system of concepts, spelling out the entire structure of means and ends within an organization.

At Kensington, a number of events took place that demanded additional labels. These include mandate, institutional plan and facade. A mandate is the formal charge or directive given by the legitimate authority. In the case of

Kensington, it is the superintendent's directive. The Institutional Plan is the particular conception of the doctrine as the principal, Mr. Shelby, had developed it prior to the August workshop. In its most articulate form, it appeared as a mimeographed document titled *Kensington Elementary School: Design for Individualized Instruction*.

In addition, Kensington's formal doctrine was codified in three other major documents: (1) the *Educational Specifications* developed for Kensington's architect, (2) a proposal to the Olds Foundation that was written by the curriculum director, and (3) a published document from the Architectural Design Institute (ADI) that described Kensington as an innovative school. In general, a high degree of consistency existed among these statements; however, each carried the slant of its particular purposes and authors.

An additional and important phrasing of the formal doctrine occurs in what we have called the facade, the formal doctrine as it was presented to the public. Even here further distinctions are required. The "public" is multiple; it includes the parents who are the immediate patrons of the school, the residents of the Milford School District, the broader audience of the subcommunities in the metropolitan area in which Milford exists and to which it compares itself and, also, the national community, which received images of Kensington through national magazines. In addition, one can discriminate between the lay audience and the professional audience, the latter being the numbers of educational personnel who visited Kensington, who heard about the school from the many spokesmen connected with it, or who read about it in the numerous professional articles that have been printed about the school.

Finally, one must speak of individual faculty member's conceptions or schemas. The school was many and sometimes different things to individual faculty members. As we shall learn, to some it was a reason for being, a total existence; for others it was mainly team teaching, or ungradedness, or individualized instruction. In effect, particular elements were abstracted and focused on by particular staff members.

As one asks oneself the question, "Why make such distinctions?" a number of answers occur. First, the doctrine varied in the world of Kensington. Second, the facade, that part which appeared in the national magazines, was often a series of specieal instances and fond hopes rather than the reality of the new school. Third, the principal's Institutional Plan was a culmination of considerable personal thought and was his image of what the school was to be made into through day-to-day interaction. It was not to be changed easily. Fourth, the doctrine served to buoy up spirits when the reality flagged. Fifth, the mandate from the superintendent to the faculty, "built a school", was in partial conflict with the principal's Institutional Plan, which had many aspects already indicated. Sixth, the individual staff conceptions, in accenting specific elements, often raised issues of conflict with the totality or other specific but different elements that another accented. Finally, and perhaps most important, the formal doctrine, especially in a new and developing school, suggest the means-means and means-ends relationships that become the structure of the school. In one sense, it is through varying interpretations, perceptions, and adaptations of doctrine that organizational structures are elaborated and changed.

SOURCES, MANIFESTATIONS, AND CONTENT OF THE DOCTRINE

The Mandate

In our theoretical analysis the initial mandate, or general set of directives issued to the principal and faculty, proceeds the formal doctrine of the school and also specifies elements in the doctrine. The mandate was characterized, as observed in the superintendent's statements, by its long-range goals. Both in substance and goals, the mandate reflects what might be called the "new elementary education" of the 1960s. The doctrine developed and adopted by the Kensington School faculty was geared somewhat more to immediacy and to effecting a program at the beginning of the school year in September.

Much of the broader mandate of the Milford School District was presented by the superintendent at a total Kensington School faculty meeting on August 18. Some of the points noted below form a major part of the doctrine that was propagated and that performed various functions for the school. The ideas were a part of a five-year plan that contained several points. In outline form, from our notes, we find the superintendent saying.

Curriculum. The curriculum is all pupil experiences while under the direction and supervision of the school. It depends on the goals and the kinds of adults we want. For example, we don't necessarily want adults who can name all 50 states, or 36 presidents, or who said the prayer in the Continental Congress. We want adults who have developed effective language techniques, life-long habits of continuous learning, and values which guide them as individuals and as members of society. We need communication and computation skills. Outside this there is no continuity. There is no instructional curriculum. We don't need to teach American history at fifth grade or individual states at fourth grade. The curriculum is determined by the needs of pupils. We don't need a crutch such as a text. We are looking for ways of organizing curriculum at Kensington School. The faculty will do this. There are no policies, no regulations, no gimmicks for you to use as an excuse. You are to determine it. The faculty is the curriculum.

Methods. (1) Individualize, (2) humanize, (3) dramatize,

(4) socialize. Under the category of individualize, one must decide how to set objectives, plan, prepare, communicate, and evaluate and in doing these decide whether or not one is operating within the framework of the group or individual. Item two, humanize, refers to getting to know the students and respecting them.

Included in dramatizing, one emphasizes creativity, divergent thinking, and devices for handling wrong answers. Socializing deals with the learning of various roles for working in groups. The past week of group development (that is, the August T-groups) contributes to this.

Time. (1) *The school day.* These should be varied lengths of time in the school day. In the elementary school some should come at 7:00, 8:00 and 9:00 and leave at 2:00, 3:00 and so forth. It is hoped that in the Kensington School there will be no bell and pupils can come when they want. We hope everyone will not leave at 3:30. (2) *The school year.* The twelve-months school year is advocated. The three months' vacation has outlived its usefulness. As an example, parents' vacations fit individual wants; they are able to resume their work when they return.

Student Ages. Two- three-, and four-year-olds should be able to come to and leave the school at varied times. All should not remain in school the same number of year.

Personnel. (1) *Teachers.* The teachers are to break down walls and become learning consultants rather than the traditional dispensers of information. (2) *Pupils.* Instead of classroom units, there will be pupil units. There will not be 18 units of 30, but 550 units. It is to be a completely individualized program. There are to be multi-level materials.

Protected Subculture : The idea of the Kensington School as a protected subculture. If we are to be change agents, we must develop subcultures. Group norms and pressures influence teachers. This subculture will protect good teachers from being influenced by group norms. By protecting subcultures, we may help the spread of ideas.

The presentation concluded with a quotation, "A man's reach should exceed his grasp or else what's heaven for?" Thus, this was the mandate and framework within which the principal and faculty at Kensington proceeded to formulate their mode of operation. As consultant Roberts viewed it, and in his words, "This is a very peculiar charge: 'Go start a new school', not 'Here are the books, go teach;" In a most important sense the new elementary education was endorsed strongly by the superintendent. It should be pointed out also that the "start a new school" interpretation is even more open ended than were the illustrative items of content themselves as they were presented by Spanman. An implicit unasked and unanswered question remained: "Is the first priority on the configuration of the content of the mandate as presented by "Spanman or on the resources of the staff members?"

Behind the superintendent's words of August 18 were earlier aspects of the intellectual content of Kensington. In January, the year before the opening of school, a district-wide proposal of the Milford schools was submitted to the Olds Foundation. Broadly stated, it was a three-years "comprehensive project for developing a design for learning." To better understand the development of Kensington's doctrine, we review briefly the purposes of the proposed project. The included these statements:

1. To reconstruct all areas of content into concepts, skills and values.
2. To develop experiences that will implement the learning of concepts, skills and values.
3. To investigate the changed roles of students and teachers in the school; that is, to change the relationship

of teachers and pupils from one of dependence to one of self-realization.

4. To decrease the time lag between the theoretical acceptance of proven new developments and the working acceptance of new developments in learning experiences.
5. To develop a comprehensive rationale of criteria necessary to initiate change in an educational enterprise.

The project was to be in three stages. In Stage I, Kensington was to be one of two elementary schools with a prototype program. State II, as delineated in the proposal, would apply the program in the middle grades of all elementary schools. During Stage III, the program would be established system wide, kindergarten through high school. Although Kensington was a protected subculture and had a mandate of its own, the district also was assumed to be ready for change, and Kensington was to be a vital part of that plan.

As we have presented it, the mandate is a concrete and tangible part of Kensington's environment. As such, the mandate is important information for the organization and for its administrator. It ties an organization or system to the larger organization. Furthermore, and to anticipate a later discussion, the mandate aids in clarifying the "supportive-non-supportive" dimension of the environment. As organizational alternatives are raised, explored, and evaluated, the mandate is the template indicating which alternatives will be supported, which will be rejected, or which will be responded to with lukewarm interest. We consider this an important specification of Simon's (1957) point that the next higher level of the larger organization specifies the decision premises of the immediately lower level of the organization. The implications for hierarchical control, for democratic school administration, and for teacher-pupil relations are quite real and quite important.

The Building Specifications

Another aspect and source of the doctrine of the Kensington School developed from the "Specs", the *Building Specifications*. We make an analysis of this document into its social psychological components. From this we can view particularly the interplay of early conceptions of the program and the physical plant as they lead to the more general point of view of the school. In the building specifications the original rationale for the design is stated straightforwardly, although abstractly: "the ultimate goal is to enable all the children of all the people to develop to the limits of their potentiality. The educational program and the physical structure facilitate this. The program changes because society changes. The building remains; hence, it must be flexible and adaptable" (pp. 1-2). The statements reflect the special concern of the architect who is aware of the open-system qualities of an educational organization and the closed-system qualities of a structure made of concrete and steel. Even so, further ambiguity is introduced because of professional education's inability to speak precisely about the ends of educational endeavours.

Objectives. The general objectives are stated and restated a number of times in the *Specifications*. The words used vary considerably: (1) "...all the children of all the people to develop to the limits of their potentiality"; (2) "...complete living in all phases of life"; (3) "...become and architect of his own character"; (4) "...self-realization"; (5) "...development of the child intellectually, socially, emotionally and physically".

The unique objectives of the school approach specificity in a statement from the *Specs:*

"The specific objectives of the educational program are: (1) to promote self-realization of the child by developing an inquiring mind; (2) to teach the basic fundamentals of reading, writing, speaking and listening in the native tongue; (3) to learn the basic concepts of numbers and calculations; (4) to achieve habits of good health and citizenship; (5) to understand the use and influence of science at present and its implications for the future; (6) to develop an appreciation for beauty in art, literature, music and nature; (7) to develop and guide children in the wise use of leisure time; (8) to inculcate an aesthetic appreciation and understanding of our cultural and spiritual values; (9) to develop self-respect and respect for human relationships towards friends, classmates, family, society and its institutions and laws; (10) to take pride in good workmanship and choice of occupation: (11) to be able to assume responsibility and cooperative effectively as a person within a group or society; (12) to develop maturity and insight in making decisions and in interpreting ideas".

Objectives are ends of human endeavour. Such a simple statement belies the complexities lying within it. In our analysis we were struck by several aspects of objectives: (1) the ends have a time dimensions varying from the present to the distant future, the oft-cited long-range and short-term quality; (2) activities can be classified as specific subgoals; (3) present activities can be classified as subgoals instrumental to distant goals; (4) goals vary on a generality-specificity continuum; (5) objectives differ in the degree to which they are written and formalized; (6) as goals become more specific, concrete, and immediate, agreement among individuals and groups of individuals becomes more difficult; (7) priorities among educational ends are not clear, and the criteria and mechanisms for establishing priorities and resolving conflict are not clear.

That these problems are not unique to Kensington is clear from Simon's statement:

> "The fact that goals may be dependent for their force on other more distant ends leads to arrangement of these goals in a hierarchy—each level to be considered as an end relative to the levels below it and as a means relative to the levels above it. Through the hierarchical structure of ends, behavior attains integration and consistency, for each member of a set of behavior alternatives is then weighed in terms of a comprehensive scale of values—the "ultimate" ends. In actual behavior, a high degree of conscious integration is seldom attained. Instead of a single branching hierarchy, the structure of conscious motives is usually a tangled web or, more precisely, a disconnected collection of elements only weakly and incompletely tied together; and the integration of these elements becomes progressively weaker as the higher levels of the hierarchy—the more final ends—are reached".

If our analysis is correct, the difficult is specification of goals in time and concreteness by the original planning group, by the superintendent, and by the principal has enabled us to move only tentatively to comparabilities in discussion of the building structure, the program of educational activities, and the structure of interaction among the significant participants. Educational and social theory have important problems that remain to be solved.

Physical facilities. In our analytic framework the statement of general and specific objectives must be accompanied by a statement of means that have high probabilities of reaching the ends. The program of activities, the interactional structural of pupils, teachers and staff, and the building facilities provide a simple taxonomy for the analysis of means. The most general statement of the building dimension appears in the *Specifications:* "Consequently, a physical plan which is considerably different from and more comprehensive than the traditional elementary plant is required". The specific elaboration of this as a taxonomy of facilities in the *Specifications* does not suggest to us more comprehensiveness or greater difference from most school plant specifications. In outline form the statement is as follows:

1. Educational Spaces
   a. General purpose classrooms
   b. Special instructional areas
2. Auxiliary Spaces
3. Special Facilities
4. General Environment.

In the analysis of educational space, the most pertinent comment for our purposes proceeds in this manner:

"In developing a design for the general purpose classroom a number of functions which are to be served by this space should be kept in mind. These functions are: 'home base' activities such as pupil accounting, guidance, individual schedule assignment, and storage of clothing; individual formal work; group formal work; individual informal work; and group informal activity".

At this point in the *Building Specifications* the analysis of interactional or organizational structure ("formal to informal work," individual to group work, and the interrelationships between the two) has arisen with mostly implicit relationships to the objectives. There has been no justification of these kinds of structures through linking the structures to the objectives. The closest of planners come to explicitness is the following introductory comment.

"Educational spaces should be designed for learning

rather than for teaching. This is a way of pointing out that many of the things which have been taught in the elementary schools have not been learned. It is not true that much has been learned that no one intended to teach. Some of these latter things such as learning to dislike the school situation, and learning to live in an adult-dominated situation while being exposed to information about democracy, have been all too common".

The special instructional areas included drama, art, music, physical education, large group activity, and the instructional materials centre. The discussion of auxiliary facilities, special facilities, and general environment does not provide clear discriminations for the present investigators. In general, the items seem to involve attention to basic physical needs of the food, clothing, and shelter variety, and include food services, toilet facilities, temperature and lighting control and the like. They do provide, however, an occasion for the educational specifications committee to introduce another general interactional variable, "the teaching-learning process."

Flexibility is stated as a key dimension in the Kensington School specifications. This conceptual label possesses several different, and it is used in several different arguments. The essential ingredient in the definition seems to be case of change. A flexible building, then, is a building that can be changed easily. Presumably, the changes are instituted in terms of vaiying purposes. The prospectus speaks of four kinds of flexibility: (1) daily flexibility, (2) frequent flexibility, (3) infrequent flexibility, (4) long-range flexibility. The first refers to day-to-day changes residing in items such as movable furniture and equipment and movable walls or partitions. The middle two categories are the ones that imply change for periods of days or weeks, and the latter category implies major and more permanent additions, deletions and alterations.

Daily flexibility becomes critical in the momentary planning by teachers and pupils. As teachers have multiple purposes and as they try to attain them in the same physical locale, then the facility needs to be flexible. Similarly, as teachers change their goals, flexible facilities are advantageous. The ability to make additions onto the building to handle increased enrollments would be an example of long-range flexibility. One might question whether Kensington's shape and internal design would permit this kind of addition. Presumably, a building may have a high degree of one kind of flexibility and a low degree of other kinds.

Social structure. Social structure, in its initial formulation, is primarily an activity structure and an interactional structure. Certain kinds of tasks are carried out and certain relationships exist among the persons involved. The building specifications suggest at several points the nature of the dimensions involved and their presumed interrelationships. We have diagramed in Figure 1.1 the relationship among general environmental conditions, the social psychological variables of groups, and individual outcomes.

Also from the *Specs*, we have abstracted references to other social psychological variables that presumably interrelate with building structure facilitate the earlier stated goals. They include organizational formats "not restricted to the traditional grade lines of K to 6". This is an early acknowledgment of the non-graded structures that were to be made concrete in the three divisions: Basic Skills, Transition, and ISD. In the *Specs* clear demarcations are not made into our broad categories of activity structure and interaction structure. Rather, a half dozen more specific interpretations are made that define the social structure of the school:

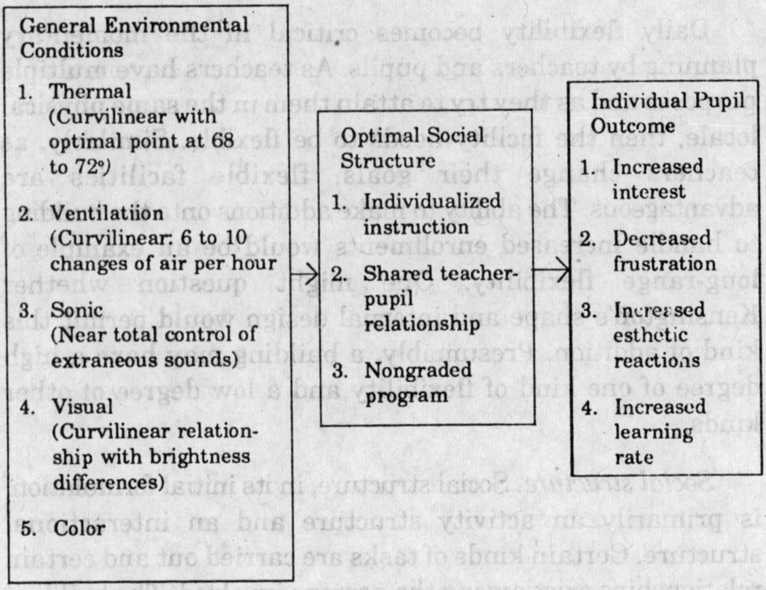

Figure 1.1. Assumed relationships between physical facilities (general environmental conditions), social psychological variables, and individual pupil outcomes.

1. "...a program flexible enough to provide for individual differences of pupils."
2. "... schedules arranged according to needs and interests of each pupil."
3. "... guidance of pupils into experiences of successful living."
4. "Purposes and methods will be shared by pupils and teachers."
5. "Pupils will carry out projects individually as well as in small groups and large groups."
6. "Learning assignments will be individualized..."

Notice that organizational structures such as team teaching receive to mention in the *Specs*. Verbs such as inform, explain, instruct, and tell also are noticeably less prominent in the *Specs* than nouns such as projects and activities. Thus, guides for teacher activity and interaction structures that presumably would facilitate planning and development of flexible programs, schedules, grouping of pupils, and individualized learning were not explicit in the specifications.

The Institutional Plan

Introduction. The "Institutional Plan" was the design of the school in the mind of the principal. The observers first heard of it in the preworkshop discussions they had in getting the research underway. The staff became aware during the middle of T-group week. The summary notes reflected the observer's interpretation at the time.

Eugene's comments about the school really came like a blast at lunch yesterday. His feelings about the "Institutional Plan" and the continual reiteration of this raised skepticism, at least, in a few of the people. This I would Judge partly by the expressions on their faces and partly by the later comments, for instance, one of the staff's asking about how flexible the Institutional Plan is. I keep getting a very strong image of Eugene as someone who wants to be a democratically oriented school administrator and, yet, who has an ego-involved idea that he sees as more vital and more real and more ideal than anything else that might be arrived at. In this sense he seems to be a man with more faith in his own idea (which is a very interesting and very exciting one, I think) than in the possibility of this group of people arriving at a better Institutional Plan. Most of this we won't really know about until next week when the individuals start working in their areas and elements of the plan become upon for interpretation in the light of very specific things that must be implemented with the pupils. For instance, one staff member has already made some digs, on occasion in the group, about the notion of effective or "fully functioning" children. She equates this conception with a bland adjustment concept and a denial of individual idiosyncrasies. I would guess that other staff also have some special interpretations here (8/12).

The ten-page statement traced briefly the history of some of the purposes and methods of education in the United States. In this account, historical interpretations were made. For instance, in the early 19th century personal instruction was used to prepare limited numbers of children for secondary education. It was in the latter part of the 19th century, with the coming of the mass education philosophy, that group instruction developed. Operating this way, the needs of the individual pupil were subordinated to efficient school administration and organization. In the 20th century more individualized, flexible programs, that were achieved by grouping based on the rate of learning, were tried. These programs were in response to the limitations of the group approach to teaching. We notice that Shelby, writing in the Institutional Plan, felt that these programs had hampered a more broadly conceived individualized instruction at the elementary school level.

Attempts which have been made to individualize instruction have concentrated on rate of learning and have failed to take into account the entire teaching-learning situation which includes talents, needs, interests, readiness, backgrounds, and motivation of students, as well as effective instructional materials and methods.

"Subjects have been presented in isolation with little or no emphasis upon interrelatedness of areas of instruction".

We now give a resum of the content of the Institutional Plan of the Kensington School. This is what was presented to visiting educators, parents, reporters, and other interested persons. Also, as we have indicated, this particularly document served as the staff's first formal contact with the new school's program.

Objectives and assumptions. The general objectives of the elementary school formulated in the plan were these:

"1. To assist pupils to become fully functioning mature human beings.
2. To meet the needs of individual differences by providing a differentiated program (rather than merely a differentiated rate for progressing through a uniform program).
3. To provide the skills, the structures, and the understandings which will enable pupils to identify worthwhile goals for themselves, and to work independently toward their attainment".

The school's function, according to the plan, was to establish and to implement a program that would assist in reaching the goals or objectives. Accordingly, the instructional program was based on two assumptions. The first idea was the learning results only from experience. Experience was defined as "what happened with an individual as a consequence of his living in or transacting with his environment." A second assumption was that it is impossible to structure a particular experience; only the environment can be structured in such a way that the desired experience is likely to occur. These assumptions implied that the Kensington School had a two-fold task: decisions must be made as to experiences considered desirable for the pupil, and ways must be located for structuring the learning environment so that these experiences are likely to evolve. The pupils at the Kensington School were to take active parts in both of processes.

There was to ben no one central focus such as textbook-centeredness, pupil-centeredness, or teacher-centeredness;

instead, numerous facets of the school were to shape the learning environment. Learning was viewed as an interactive process that varied from individual to individual. These ideas were a part of the rationale utilized in decision-making as it related to curriculum, teacher-pupil roles, the organization of the school, the building and facilities, and the instructional materials.

Curriculum. The Kensington School placed primary emphasis on process development as opposed to content development. What was designated as the "spiral curriculum" in which concepts, skills, and values were the central elements aided in this shift in emphasis. The document stated that:

> "Concepts, skills, and values form the unifying threads around which learning experiences are provided. Referred to as the 'spiral curriculum', this approach places major emphasis on process development rather than content development. Although ample provision is made for individualization of the curriculum, continuity, sequence, and integration of knowledge are facilitated through the use of curriculum guides which have been developed. Since organization of knowledge really takes place in the mind of the learner, the structure of the curriculum does not determine directly what is learned by pupils, but influences learning indirectly through helping to shape the learning 'milieu' for pupils".

Later, and in considerable detail, we shall present the staff's attempts to translate these ideas into day-to-day events in the lives of the children.

Redefinition of teacher-pupil roles. The document emphasized that more was involved in accomplishing the objectives of the school than just slicing subject matter in a variety of ways. The contributions of the behavioral sciences to a recognition of vital human forces in the teaching-learning process that are of concern when planning educational programs were cited. Human factors such as motivation, perception, discipline, communication, and thinking were designated as important in the acquisition of knowledge as well as in the development of the pupils into fully-functioning human beings, which it will be remembered was one of the general objectives. The application of these processes brought about the recognition of a need for a change in the traditional teacher-pupil roles and in the organizational climate in which this interaction occurs. Figure 1.2 shows the change in emphasis in teacher-pupil roles.

From	*To*
Passive, reactive pupils	Active, initiating pupils
Pupil followership	Pupil leadership
Restriction of pupils	Freedom for pupils
External motivation	Self-discipline Self-motivation
Group activities	Individual activities
Restricting pupil interaction	Encouraging pupil interaction
Teacher responsibility for teaching	Pupil responsibility for learning
Teacher planning	Teacher-pupil planning
Teacher evaluation	Teacher-pupil evaluation
Teacher as a dispenser of knowledge	Teacher as catalyst for inquiry
Teacher as controller of pupils	Teacher as organizer for learning
Identical roles for teachers	Differentiated roles for teachers
Closed, rigid social climate	Open, flexible social climate.

Figure 1.2 The Institutional Plan's redefinition of teacher-pupil roles.

Although our field notes contain no staff references to the work of H. H. Anderson and his colleagues, and the Institutional Plan does not footnote their contributions (1945, 1946a, 1946b), it seems fair to say that the redefinition of teacher-pupil roles is congruent with Anderson's continuum of dominative to integrative social contacts between teachers and children. Similarly, the pupil behaviors of spontaneity, self-initiation, and activity are within his conceptual framework. In the second-to-last item in Figure 1.2 the shift from identical to differentiated teachers' roles is a new element introduced, but even here Anderson's conception of "inviting differences" seems relevant.

Organization of the Kensington School. "Organization of teachers and pupils assumes a different perspective when viewed in terms of implementing a new approach to the attainment of refocused objectives. As with all other elements of the school, organization is merely (designed-intended) for the purpose of facilitating the educational program. The appropriateness of the form of organization employed is dependent upon the function of the school".

The doctrine surrounding the organization stresses flexibility. Teacher-pupil organization has as its base "planned flexibility." "Both horizontal and vertical organization of the school are, therefore, designed to provide the framework within which is possible the frequent reorganization of pupils and teachers for meaningful instructional activities". Vertical organization is considered as referring to the sequence of progression through the school and is closely related to the concept of gradedness. In the past, in most schools sequence has not been viewed as problematic; however, the failure elsewhere to recognize that there are numerous sequences is pointed out in the document. The Kensington School avoids organizing on the basis of "rigidly defined 'levels' " or six lock-step grades. The vertical organization has three basic divisions, and there is opportunity for flexibility within and between divisions. The three divisions—Basic Skills, Transition, and Independent Study (ISD)—are planned to perform differentiated functions. The organization within, horizontal organization, is also differentiated for maximum effectiveness. Much of this is summarized in a summary from the Institutional Plan.

As has been shown, much of the doctrine emphasized the flexibility of both the building and the instructional program. The provision for individual differences of students to the extent of schedules arranged according to the needs and interests of each pupil, which represented the "highly individualized" program, was descriptive of the school's intentions.

Schemas of Individual Faculty Members

In effect, we have presented a number of instances of the formal doctrine as individual conceptions, since the mandate reflected the superintendent's position, the foundation request was written primarily by the curriculum director, and the Institutional Plan was the principal's formal statement of his view of the doctrine. However, the data suggest strongly, as will a reading of later descriptive aspects of this monograph, that each faculty member held has own view or schema of Kensington. Typically, each schema seemed to be generated out off personal needs and goals, early conversations about the school (especially with Spanman and Shelby), and early documents. As the faculty convinced in August, the individual and common experiences of each seemed to shape the conceptions a step or two further. As the divisions and teams went their individual ways, both geographically and instructionally, individual members were privy to only partial experiences of the totality. The channels of informal communication were interlocked through living arrangements, for example, one of the Basic Skills-4 team members lived with an ISD teacher and another lived with a Transition teacher. Although these circumstances, and devices such as monthly Saturday morning staff meetings and frequent staff bulletins, served communication functions, people saw and heard only limited parts of the totality. The researchers were frequently the object of "What's going on overt at...?" type of questions. Most of these questions were parried with a variety of responses. For example: "Why? What have you heard?"

MANIFESTATIONS, CONTENT, DIMENSIONS AND CONSEQUENCES OF

Perhaps, the most critical doctrinal outcome for the organization was the inability of a number of the individual conceptions to become merged into a common enough framework, an agreed on interpretation of the doctrine. Individual and subgroup interpretations of this doctrine were involved as we report shortly in the early schism between the two teams in Basic Skills, in the coalition aspects of Transition, and in the continuing conflict in ISD. Differences as to teaching methods, materials, pupil control, and staff organization were prevalent. The staff was verbal and articulate in isolating and elaborating "reasonable but incompatible" individual interpretations of what Kensington should stand for. As these intertwined with other personality variables and with episodes in the school's evolving social processes (such as the T-groups), they contributed to the complex puzzle that was Kensington. These processes are diagramed in Figure 1.3.

Summary

In a sense, we are caught between these different but highly overlapping statements. On the one hand, they were sources of the formal doctrine; on the other hand, they were statements of it. In effect, there was no one clear and totally accepted statement of the doctrine. As we cite in other parts of our analysis, even more variety occurred in the conceptions of the doctrine as they were held by individual staff members. As in the parable, the elephant was less than an elephant as the five man clutched it in the dark, and thus it was as the faculty members viewed the Kensington Schools.

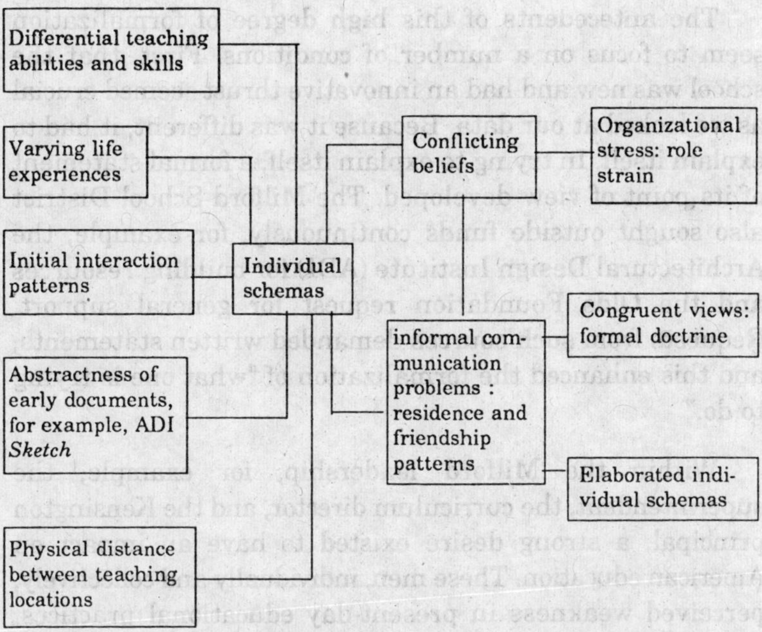

Figure 1.3 The antecedents and consequences of individual faculty schemas of Kensington doctrine

STRUCTURAL DIMENSIONS OF THE DOCTRINE

As we analyze the doctrine apart from its substantive content, several structural dimensions seem significant. They include the degree of formalization, the degree of abstractness, the degree of consistency, and the degree of effectively.

Formalization. We have described in detail the nature and content of the Kensington "point of view", its formal doctrine. As we tried to formulate the conception in terms of a continuum, we found that the rephrasing as formalized doctrine, the degree to which the "point of view" is systematized and codified, seemed significant. Kensington had a high degree of this formalization. Presumably, some schools have a considerably less articulated doctrine.

The antecedents of this high degree of formalization seem to focus on a number of conditions. First, that the school was new and had an innovative thrust seemed crucial as we looked at our data. Because it was different, it had to explain itself. In trying to explain itself, a formal statement of its point of view developed. The Milford School District also sought outside funds continuously, for example, the Architectural Design Institute (ADI) for building resources and the Olds Foundation request for general support. Requests from such sources demanded written statements, and this enhanced the formalization of "what one is trying to do."

Within the Milford leadership, for example, the superintendent, the curriculum director, and the Kensington principal, a strong desire existed to have an impact on American education. These men, individually and collectively, perceived weakness in present-day educational practices. They had vivid images of a better mode of operation. Not only did they seek to put these into practice, but also they talked and wrote about their ideas. Such behavior helped to shape a more formalized doctrine. Also, and particularly within the Kensington faculty. Shelby had strong codifying and analytical motivation. He tried to make conscious a wide realm of school activity.

Finally, we saw the community conflict as an important aspect of the move toward a formalized doctrine. The Milford District had a reputation for many years as a community that has fought over its school program. Tentatively, we would argue that the superintendent's early attempts to build a social base at the district level pushed him to verbalize and codify his position. Later, Shelby was forced in this same way by the patrons of the school who wanted to know "what was going on?"

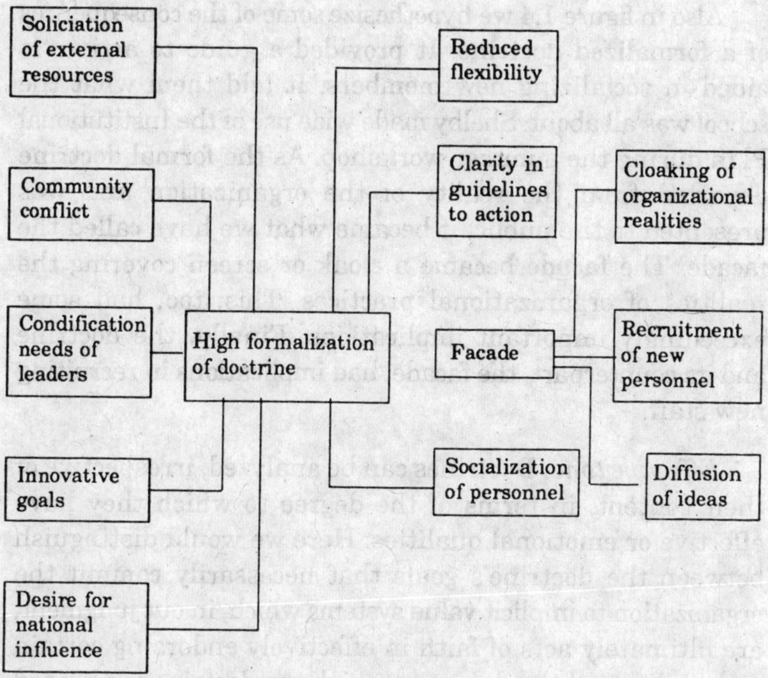

Figure 1.5. The implications of the formalization of the doctrine.

These relations have been sketched in Figure 1.4.

Although he was commenting on TVA, Selznick seemed to capture the interrelationships among the several sources of the doctrine as they were part of Kensington.

"This quest for an ideology, for doctrinal nourishment, while general, to uneven. Organizations established in a stable context, with assured futures, do not feel the same urgencies as those born of turmoil and set down to fend for themselves in undefined ways among institutions fearful and resistant. As in individuals, insecurity summons ideological reinforcements. The TVA was particularly susceptible to this kind of insecurity because it was not the spontaneous product of the institutions in its area of operation".

Also in figure 1.4 we hypothesize some of the consequences of a formalized doctrine. It provided a guide to action. It aided in socializing new members. It told them what the school was all about. Shelby made wide use of the Institutional Plan during the summer workshop. As the formal doctrine departed from the reality of the organization and was presented to the public, it became what we have called the facade. The facade became a cloak or screen covering the realities of organizational practices. This, too, had some exceedingly important implications. Finally, the doctrine and its counterpart, the facade, had implications in recruiting new staff.

Effective tone. Doctrines can be analyzed, irrespective of their content, in terms of the degree to which they have effective or emotional qualities. Here we would distinguish between the doctrine's goals that necessarily commit the organization to implicit value systems which, in our judgment, are ultimately acts of faith in effectively endorsing certain ends in life and the degree to which the doctrine is phrased in terms of emotional appeals that seek to persuade on irrelevant or highly tenuous grounds. Operationally, we presume one might measure doctrinal documents on this effective-tone dimension by engaging in content analysis, using as a format the usually described propagandistic emotional appeals.

In the Institutional Plan, the principal's document, the affective tone is present but moderate, at least, in comparison to the Architectural Design Institute's (ADI) account. For instance, the former states as a conclusion:

> "Rather than organizing on the basis of six lock-step grades, or even greater number of rigidly defined 'levels', as many 'non-graded' schools do, the vertical organization of Kensington Elementary School consists of three basic divisions with ample opportunity for flexibility between

and within these divisions. Referred to as the Basic Skills Division, Transition Division, and Independent Study Division, these organizational units are designed to serve differentiated functions. The horizontal organization, or organization within each division, is consequently differentiated for maximum effectiveness".

Similarly Figure 1.2, the "From-To" diagram, contains a number of affectively oriented educational statements. The document from ADI contains even more significant attempts to excite the reader.

"The initial impact is embodied in the simplicity of the building design, calling forth an image of an earlier era of civilization. A Parthenon whose qualities contribute to an effect of organically articulated form rather than mere massiveness, of subtle refinement rather than gross power. A building whose shape is in fact a prototype of evolutionary progress in educational growth. It is a offering facility and speed, mobility and flexibility to a non-graded, organic, fluid approach to inquiry".

Such a glowing account, that is, a high degree of doctrinal affectivity, seems to have a number of consequences. They include, for instance, a visibility, a stimulus for enthusiasm, and a less than critical quality of thinking. We sketch a broader model of relevant hypotheses as Figure 1.5.

In short, the affective tone, especially as we have seen it in the ADI publication, and later with the appearance of the facade, suggested two important cautions to us. We have renewed our suspicions of written accounts that seem to strive to excite the reader. Also, we have renewed our concern regarding potential incongruencies between the doctrine in its many forms and the organizational reality lying beneath it.

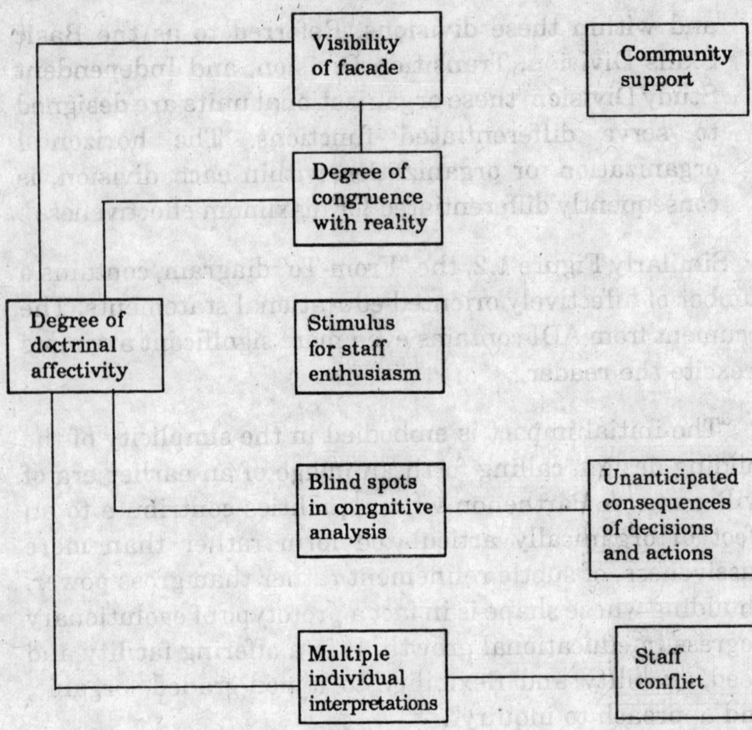

Figure 1.5. The implications of the affective tone dimensions of the formal doctrine.

Integration. The degree to which the content of the formal doctrine is consistent or integrated seems another dimension worthy of further investigation. Several illustrations proved almost classical in our observations. One of the major goals was individual pupil decision-making. A major subgoal was an organizational structure that involved team teaching. The experienced teachers reacted frequently and spontaneously that they were able to provide more individual pupil decision-making in their self-contained classrooms of prior years than they could in a team where their behavior was contingent on their teaching peers instead of upon their pupils. Relevant excerpts from the field notes appear in several parts of the report: the descriptive accounts of Kensington and the more systematic analysis of team teaching.

Another illustration of inconsistency within the doctrine appears in the deification of the group and of the individual. The doctrine argues for group consensus as an ultimate goal and individual development as an ultimate goal. The point we make here is similar to Spindler's (1955) analysis of the transformation within American culture from traditional to emergent values. Kensington had internalized within its doctrine intense commitments to values of individually and social processes. On what occasions and in what situations one value or the other took precedence was not clear. The rules about rules or norms about norms remained a critical problem throughout the year. The social and personal conflict predicted by Spindler became a part of Kensington. In effect, the doctrine was giving simultaneous and incompatible signals or directions to the teachers and provoking conflict within and between them. Neither the staff nor the broader establishment of American Education has entertained strong analytic attention to this kind of issue. In terms of testable hypotheses, we offer the model in Figure 1.6.

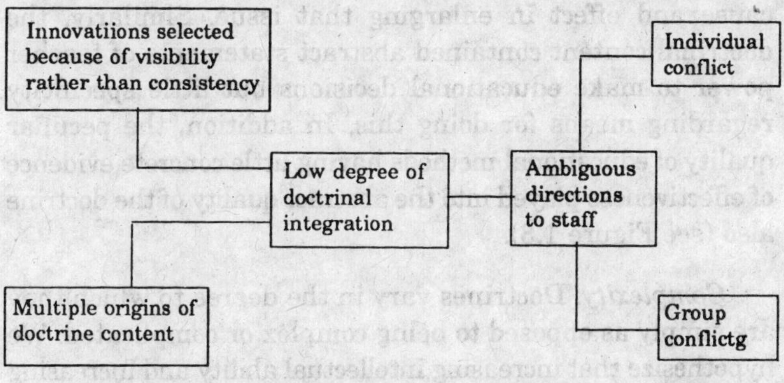

Figure 1.6. Hypotheses surrounding doctrinal integration.

Abstractness. Doctrine may vary also in the degree to which it is abstract or concrete. Kensington's doctrine accented the abstract. Issues were treated at a lofty and general level. For instance, explicit concrete definitions of "individualized instruction" and "fully-functioning pupils" did not receive final or agreed on concrete operational definitions. Individualized instruction could be a carefully guided tutorial experience in which the teacher communicated specific concepts to a single pupil, or it could be a self-selected learning experience engaged in by one or more pupils. As a language system is abstract, it permits legitimate but varying concrete interpretations. A doctrine with considerable abstractness hypothetically can provoke a wide range of these interpretations. This problem arose even when it seemed that considerable specificity had been obtained with respect to teaming, resource specialists and academic counsellors.

As we indicate shortly, Kensington had a further complication in terms of the individual faculty-member styles of problem solving. Early in the summer workshop, some members wanted to deal with "nuts and bolts" while others preferred the broader philosophical questions and an accompanying deductive strategy and tactics for problem solving. The abstractness of the doctrine seemed to be both cause and effect in enlarging that issue. Similarly, the doctrinal content contained abstract statements of teacher power to make educational decisions but little specificity regarding means for doing this. In addition, the peculiar quality of educational methods having little concrete evidence of effectiveness played into the abstract quality of the doctrine also (see Figure 1.8).

Complexity. Doctrines vary in the degree to which they are simply as opposed to being complex or complicated. We hypothesize that increasing intellectual ability and increasing compulsivity of influential group members produce an organizational point of view that has many parts, elements, and nuances. Kensington's doctrine had a number of elements and each element, for instance, the nature of pupil-teacher interaction, had a series of components listed in great detail, as we show in Figure 1.2.

Scope. Related to the complexity of the doctrine is the doctrine's pervasiveness or scope, that is, how much of organizational life is covered by the doctrine. In Kensington's case it was large. Specification in goals covered the total child and specification in procedures covered the whole day and multitude of ways of behaving—teaming, ungradeness, no textbooks, and the like. This quality of doctrine scope has implications for personal commitment to the organization by its members. The important consequences of this characteristic are amplified in a later chapter.

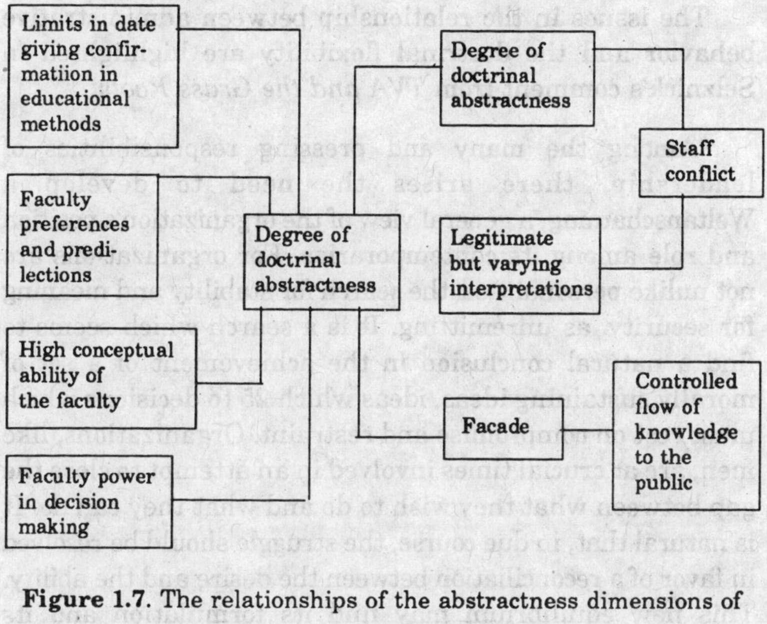

Figure 1.7. The relationships of the abstractness dimensions of the formal doctrine.

Flexibility. Flexibility has at least two kinds of subissues connected with it. One of them is the flexibility or rigidity with which individuals hold to the specific content of the doctrine. For instance, during the summer workshop early in Kensington's history, Shelby was most reluctant to depart from the Institutional Plan and to create with the faculty new and different structures. The other subissue, and a central one for the point concerning flexibility, is the degree of changeableness of the doctrine. For instance, to cloak the point in good and bad words, a doctrine that is unyielding or unchangeable is "rigid" and a doctrine which changes constantly is "overly pliant" or "vacillatory." The "right" amount of changeableness is flexible." We would hypothesize that doctrines vary in the degree to which they are changeable, and this was important consequences for the organization whose social structure and activities are changing rapidly as was that of Kensington.

The issues in the relationship between administrative behavior and the doctrinal flexibility are highlighted in Selznick's comment from *TVA and the Grass Roots*.

"Among the many and pressing responsibilities of leadership, there arises the need to develop a Weltanschauung, a general view of the organization's position and role among its contemporaries. For organizations are not unlike personalities: the search for stability and meaning for security, as unremitting. It is a search which seems to find a natural conclusion in the achievement of a set of morally sustaining ideas, ideas which 25 to decisions which must rest on compromise and restraint. Organizations, like men, are at crucial times involved in an attempt to close the gap between what they wish to do and what they can do. It is natural that, in due course, the struggle should be resolved in favor of a reconciliation between the desire and the ability. This new equilibrium may find its formulation and its sustenance in ideas which reflecta softened view of the world. The ethic of revolt, of thoroughgoing change, assumes that human and institutional materials are readily malleable and that disaffection from current modes of thought and patterns of behavior can be long sustained in action. But leadership must heed the danger of strain and disaster as recalcitrance and intertia exert their unceasing pressures; in doing so, it may see wisdom in the avowal of loyalty to prevailing codes and established structures. The choice, indeed, may often lie between adjustment and organizational suicide".

In the early spring of the year, the successes of parts of the program (especially in Basic Skills), the nourishment of enthusiasm through attention, and the Milford district-wide attempts for a large-scale curriculum project contributed to the hightening of the Curriculum Committee's activity and a return to doctrinal considerations instead of to an expenditure of energy and resources on the day-to-day programmatic aspects of instructional materials and procedures. Kensington's choice, as it were, was to *not* change the doctrine.

Uniqueness. Doctrines vary along a dimension of "run-of-the-mill" to uniqueness. As one looks at a number of schools, one can observe an important variation on this dimension. Kensington's ideology was not common-place; its point of view was unusual in the variety of ways about which we have talked a length already and that we shall discuss especially in the next chapters. A unique doctrine along with other aspects of uniqueness, for example, the physical structure of the building, makes the school visible, attracts a particular kind of staff, mobilizes energies, and may well evoke a higher ratio of unanticipated to anticipated consequences of purposive organizational activity.

CONSEQUENCES OF THE DOCTRINE

As with all of our analyses, the models specifying antecedents and consequences indicate multiple hypotheses. These relationships seem viable in our data, and we offer them as testable propositions for the realities of other educational organizations. As we developed further the analysis of the formal doctrine, it seemed to fall comfortably into the context provided by our general conception of manifest and latent functions and dysfunctions.

Manifest Functions

Guide to action. A formal doctrine contains statements of goals and objectives toward which one strives. Also it contains subgoals to be approached "on the way" toward the more general and ultimate objectives. Similarly, it contains specification of means, that is, alternatives of action, of social structure, and of procedures that contain high probabilities of attaining the goals. In effect, it is a plan—a guide to individual action and group activity. Kensington's formal doctrine possessed this manifest function. The building was built according to the building specifications. The August workshop was run according to the Institutional Plan. Although school was opened in temporary quarters, the dimensions of the beginning, as we shall describe shortly, occurred in terms of divisional and team understandings and interpretations of the doctrine. The doctrine had a potency that could not be denied. The structures fostered by the doctrine often contained a number of dysfunctions, as we discuss in detail at other points in the book.

Group norms. Formal doctrine in its ultimate sense becomes the codified policies and rules of the bureaucracy as stated in the manuals of standard operating procedures. Group norms reflect the same kinds of issues, except that they usually are the informal statements of "the way we do things around here." The congruence of these two systems has been the subject of a fair amount of research and discussion. Relatively less has been said of the interdependency in the development of each. One of the more graphic illustrations was reported by Arensberg and McGregor (1942) and reanalyzed by Homans in *The Human Group* (1950). As the "electrical equipment company" was analyzed in the latter volume, the formal organizational charts reflected an earlier period in the organization's history, but the company norms reflected the issues of a number of years of survival during difficult and complex environmental shifts (for example, the economic depression of the 1930s). The authors as consultants argued for a reshaping of the doctrine to fit the current norms and procedural activities.

At Kensington, we have the exciting case of multiple statements of the doctrine prior to the interaction of the staff and students who were to be the incumbents of the organization. These statements, especially the Institutional Plan, and the forcefulness of the principal as author of the Plan and as the central and most powerful member of the staff, provided the basic framework in which norms were to develop. The issues in the doctrine were the issues with which the faculty struggled throughout the year.

In Jackson's (1960) terms, norms did not crystallize within the staff. Staff turnover was at a high rate even before the end of the first year, for example, Kirkham was replaced and Larsen, his replacement, was temporary. Linda joined the ISD staff at mid-year. Jack became ill in the spring and was replaced for several months by Lee, a long-term substitute. Elaine was married at mid-year and left in the spring; Sarah took her place. The conflict and interpersonal difficulties contributed heavily to this lack of norm crystalization. Some subgroups did work well together and friendship groups developed also. They tended to give a picture of norm ambiguity, a special case of low crystallization.

Latent Dysfunctions

Cloaking of organizational realities. A well-codified and an abstract doctrine has a number of dysfunctions. One of them is the cloaking of organizational realities. In this usage we argue that every organization to some degree masks its internal functioning to its public. We hypothesize that the more formalized the doctrine becomes and the more internal problems that exist, the greater the degree of masking that will occur. By internal problems we mean, at Kensington, the severe staff conflict, especially in the Independent Study Division, and the difficulties the divisions had in implementing the program as defined initially. Additional impetus to the cloaking of activities was the continuous "battle" with, at least, a minority of vocal parents and district residents whose biases toward traditional education were in conflict with one or more of the innovative elements of the programs.

As consequences, inaccuracies in perception of the realities of the school and parental frustrations developed. This, in turn, prevented the building of long-term support for the school as well as for the district leadership. These implications are diagramed in Figure 1.8.

Self-deception. At least since the Freudian revolution, language systems have been viewed as possible vehicles for self-deception, rationalizations. An ideology or group belief with its concomitant social support possesses the increased strength to carry out consequences such as self-deception. In his trenchant style, Hoffer (1951) draws the picture of the extreme condition in the relation of doctrine to self-deception.

"All active mass movements strive, therefore, to interpose a fact proof screen between the faithful and the realities of the world. They do this by claiming that the ultimate and absolute truth is already embodied in their doctrine and that there is no truth or certitude outside it. The facts on which the true believer bases his conclusions must not be derived from his experience or observation but from holy writ".

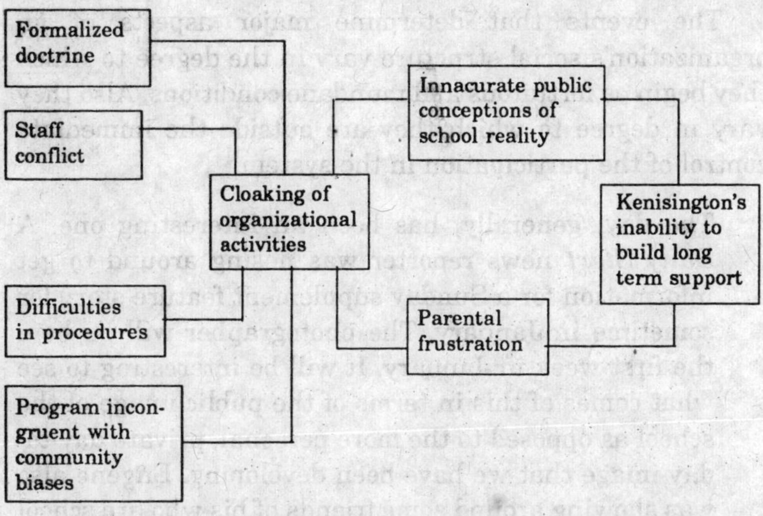

Figure 1.8. The antecedents and consequences of cloaking organizational activities.

The modal member of Kensington was not his extreme, although some individual staff members were. As we analyze in detail later in the discussion entitled. "On true belief in an innovative organization," Kensington and have such a quality about it. The formal doctrine seems to contribute to the making of reality with regard to the members of the system.

In retrospect, as we reflect on the party described in the introductory epilogue, a number of the elements described in Festinger *et al. When Prophecy Fails* (1956), seem to have occurred at Kensington. Strong belief, commitment in action, specific implementations or ties to the real world, disconfirmations, and social support were critical elements.

For at least a minority of the staff (Witness the comments by John and Jean in Chapter One) the phenomenon described by Festinger occurred.

The Facade: Functions and Dysfunctions

The events that determine major aspects of an organization's social structure vary in the degree to which they begin as fortuitous and mundane conditions. Also they vary in degree to which they are outside the immediate control of the participation in the system.

> The day, generally, has been an interesting one. A *Daily Start* news reporter was nosing around to get information for a Sunday supplement feature story for sometime in January. The photographer will be here the first week in January. It will be interesting to see what comes of this in terms of the public image of the school as opposed to the more personal, private day-to-day image that we have been developing. Engene also was showing around some friends of his who are school people in Canada. Today's Bulletin carried with it also a statement about observers in this school and the need to plan for these people and schedule them. I'm struck by the facade that they must see on these one-day shots. I quizzed the reporter as to the genesis of the story and apparently the Sunday supplement news editor lives in this part of town and has seen and been familiar with the development of the building and thought it might be a good idea. It apparently was as informal as that. He commented also that they have a difficult time getting newsworthy and particularly photography-worthy articles on schools and this one is especially appropriate for that (12/23).

As we use the concept, facade refers to the image that the school presents to the several publics. Kensington was a highly visible school. Prior to our study, the board hired a superintendent who was articulate the bright, a "comer", to use a colloquial phrase. He held strong interests in developing in the Milford School District a unique, novel, and ultra-contemporary educational program. Kensington was a major part of this. Through the consultants at ADI, and their publications, the school attained an initial visibility. Thus, the first image of the school was projected. As this attracted increased attention, further aspects of the formal doctrine were needed, were available, and were utilized to present the image of the school. As awards were won for architectural design, popular news media began to describe the program, which was equally unique. The process accelerated.

Theoretically, the uniqueness of the physical structure of the building and the superintendent's intentions for national leadership by Milford created an initial visibility. With this visibility came increased attention and the need for a codified point of view—the formal doctrine. However, as our descriptive materials will indicate, the day-to-day functioning reality was not totally congruent with the doctrine. This led to the special public face" which centered on intentions, "what we are trying to do", and on special atypical concrete instances that illustrated these intentions.

The facade produced many important outcomes. On the one hand, the local and national acclaim was a hearty stimulant to flagging faculty spirits. The newspaper and magazine accounts brought commentary about "our school" from parents, relatives and friends. The complex process of social approval and identity development for the individual staff member in relationship to his occupation of teaching seemed highly significant. The energizing aspect was noted early in January.

> Today was the day that the *Daily Star* photographer was out in the Milford School District and at Keensington. How much he was a "causal agent" I don't know and

> how much resides in the fact that I observed the Basic Skills team of four, but today the school looked and operated much more like a thriving, ongoing enterprise. As I walked in I noted that the bicycles were being put over on the side where the kids had been instructed to put them. The play area had been hosed down and was relatively clean and the heaters, except for two or three, were all working. The perception core was full of busy kids who were reading, working on reports, and active in this regard rather than fussing with the models and playing with games. The language arts program in the Basic Skills team moved readily, easily, and with a real flair, as well as seemingly with important learning outcomes for the children. As I walked out of the building. John had his mats on the stage of the play area and the kids were tumbling and were doing exercises. The photographer was taking pictures of the children with the colorful backdrop of the wall behind the staging area. Perhaps the school was just putting its best foot forward for the visitors and the photographer. Be that as it may, when the best foot forward is so put, it is a very good one (1/6).

By the cloaking of organizational realities, we have reference to a biased or partial picture of the organization. The field notes contained references of *National Weekly's* article on the school. The journalist spent a week in the school in January, and the feature article appeared in early summer after the first year of the school's operation.

> As I read the article I am struck by a feeling I had in earlier public presentations: although most of the material in the article is true, there is an erroneous conception developed through the lack of what is said. For instance, the title of the article reads "A school where children teach themselves." Without question,

> in some parts of ISD a number of children are engaged in such activities and are teaching themselves. This seems particularly true in David's and Linda's rooms. This is most certainly *not* true in the Basic Skills, in Transition, and in at least half of ISD. Similarly, the subheading of the article: "Strange things happen within this strange looking building. With teachers only leading the way, kids from 6 to 12 decide whether to do advanced math, study the philosophy of communism, or measure the diameter of the sun. Best of all, says the school, they are learning to learn." Without question, there has been some election of math, although one would need to define carefully "advanced." If this were to be applicable. Also without question, some of the children studied the philosophy of communism. And I imagine some of them discussed measuring the diameter of the sun, although I have no direct recollection of this. The majority of the children did not do any one of these three things. Among the major options, which the author did not suggest and which many of the pupils elected, were spending considerable time working with the tape records, playing with the art supplies, and passing the time of day (6/24, post-experimental year).

Other critical comments we would make on the public image are: inadequate discriminations between intention and reality in the program, the isolation of atypical teachers who were not representative of the majority, and inadequate normative data to make comparisons of the such items as frequency of discipline problems. Hypotheses concerning the sources and consequences of the facade are presented in Figure 1.9 Elements in the diagram, for example, the formal doctrine, must be integrated with prior discussion for additional antecedents and implications.

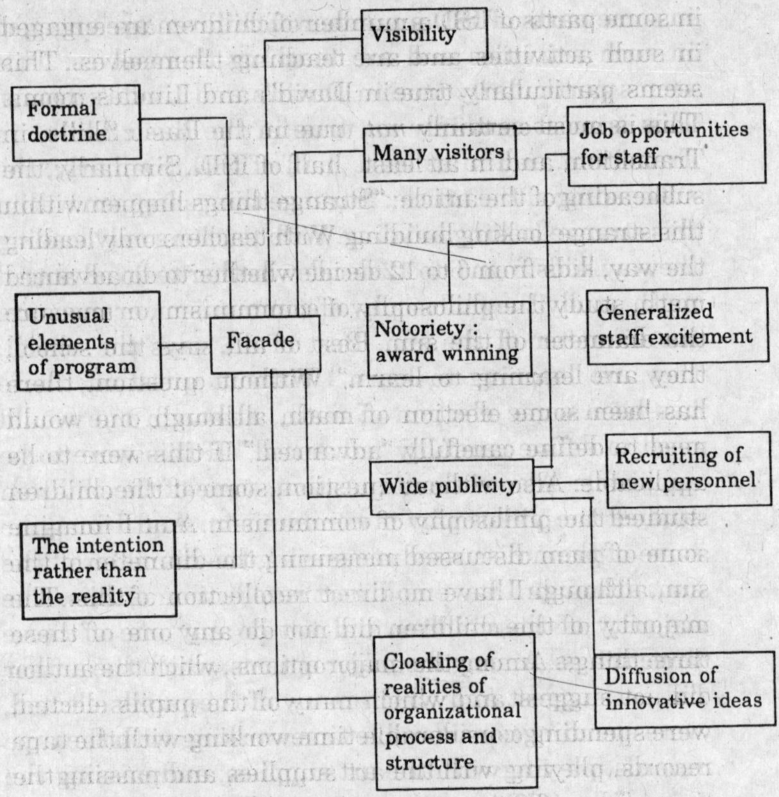

Figure 1.9. The implications of the facade.

Conclusions

Our conclusions follow simply from the description and analysis. One needs a concept such as formal doctrine to talk fully and incisively about Kensington. Presumably, schools will vary in the degree to which they possess a visionary, conscious, and codified ideology. Second, in some instances, antecedents to the doctrine will exist in the form of mandates, as with Kensington. Other schools, especially new ones, will have building specifications that play dual roles—as antecedents of doctrine and later as another manifestation and sometimes contending operational definition of the doctrine. Third, organizational positions soon possess incumbents who interpret mandates, building specifications, and foundation proposals in terms of their own cognitive maps and professional schemas. In some situations this may be formalized to the point of a written "Institutional Plan." In the instance of Kensington this was a forceful and potent position paper. As we shall see later, it was a major determinant of the principal's decision-making, a guide to the faculty, a source of conflict, and a major issue in the dilemmas of democratic administration.

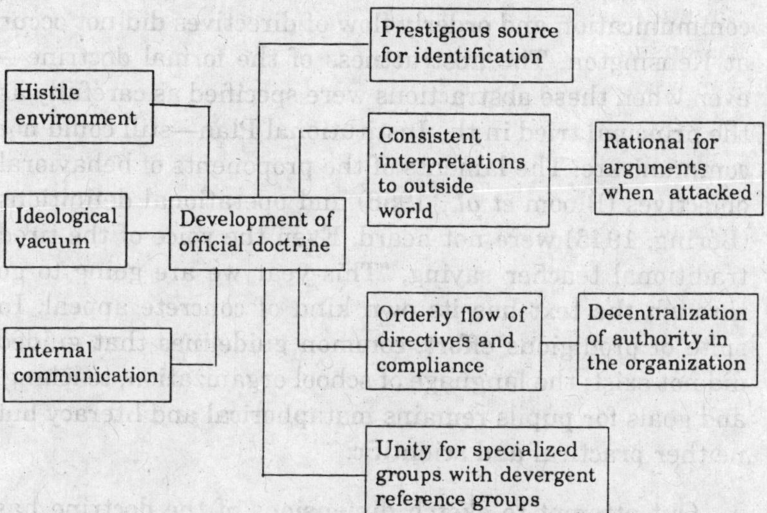

Figure 1.10. A model clarifying Selznick's reasoning concerning TVA's official doctrine.

To complement our observations and analysis we give a brief summary of Selznick's position on "official doctrine" as he presented it in his study of the Tennessee Valley Authority. This discussion we have codified in Figure 1.10. Such a model indicates similarities across organizations and is suggestive for a more extended comparative organizational theory. The genesis of the "official doctrine" lay in a hostile environment, an ideological vacuum, and a need for communication within the organization. The antecedents of Kensington's formal doctrine overlapped only partially. The consequences, too, seen only partially common.

Perhaps schools differ from regional governmental organizations, or perhaps it is innovative schools that differ from innovative regional governmental organizations. Our may be it is just Kensington and TVA that we are contrasting. Nonetheless, the doctrinal functions of internal communication and orderly flow of directives did not occur at Kensington. The abstractness of the formal doctrine—even when these abstractions were specified as carefully as the principal tried in the Institutional Plan—still could not communicate. The laments of the proponents of behavioral objectives (Bloom *et al.*, 1956) and operational definitions (Boring, 1945) were not heard. Even the voice of the tired traditional teacher saying, "This year we are going to go through the text has its own kind of concrete appeal. In spite of prodigious effort, common guidelines that guided did not exist; the language of school organization, teaching, and goals for pupils remains mataphorical and literacy but neither practical and scientific.

Out attempt to sketch dimensions of the doctrine has been exploratory, yet influential in our own thinking. As we have stated at a number of points our models seem to reflect well many of the specifics of our case. The degree to which they are more generally true awaits systematic verificational research. However, to the educational administrator to whom this book is, in part, directed, we urge that he think this way through his problems with an eye altered to dimensions similar to ours and with this ear tuned for latent consequences similar to the ones we found.

Finally, we think the facade concept is most important. The organizational face presented to the public—especially in popular newspapers and magazines—did not reflect the reality of the school. These discrepancies have led us toward skepticism and caution with respect to any "feature" story about educational matters. Administrators who seriously try to keep up with the Jones District—or its facade—seem to be creating a new kind of problem while they are attempting to solve the original one.

2

Conceptualizing Organizational Origins and Development

Tucked away in a volume on leadership as statesmanship, Selznick (1957) presents a brief discussion of three developmental problems in the origins of an Organizations: the selection of a social base, the building of an institutional core, and the formalization of procedure. These tasks confront the organization with initial and critical policy decisions. For our analysis, they provide us with an introduction to the origins of organizational development. Selznick comments in regard to the first conception:

> "The early phase of an institution's life is marked by a scrutiny of its own capabilities, and of its environment, to discover where its resources are and on whom it is dependent. The achievement of stability is influenced by this appraisal; and the future evolution of the institution is largely conditioned by the commitments generated in this basic decision".

With respect to Kensington, we shall have more to say as we analyze the school's relationship to "the everpresent environment." For the moment, we would indicate that the lot of Kensington was cast with Spanman, the new superintendent; and his assistant, Cohen, the curriculum, director. Shelby, the principal, was part of the new guard of

Milford, and his school was a major element in the new program. The dependency here was so great that the superintendent's departure, a temporary one-year leave that later became permanent, and the curriculum director's departure at the end of the first year were mortal blows. Although no one knew it at the time, one might argue that was the moment that Kensington died. Characteristic of the "typical" employee or incumbent in an organizational position. The task "rises above ordinary life because it requires one to leave business-as-usual and commit himself earnestly to something he believes in deeply" (Klapp, p. 257). The uniqueness, the separateness, the differentness, the intensity of the sentiments and behaviors of the individual engaged in an enterprise of this kind must be emphasized. Thus, it is both the remedial effort with its extraordinary intents and the accompanying zeal and enthusiasm that hep define the role of the crusader. As such, this corresponds to Hoffer's concept of true belief.

Kensington exemplified well how a crusade may differ from a movement aimed at only practical results. At one level the school was a program organized to institutionalize the "new elementary education." At another, it was a movement to develop and to extend a set of beliefs surrounding change processes in general and elementary education in particular. It is at the latter level that the elements of a crusade are most clearly illustrated.

Aspects of true belief were formalized in various elements of the doctrine and facade, as we have indicated previously. In this way, true belief and its concomitants extend beyond any practical attempt and are maintained in the face of failure. Although a part of the crusader's role, if he is engaged in a demonstration of his ideas, may be to bring the reality in line with his stated attempts, the facade incorporates the hopes and dreams that the humdrum of the mundane may deteriorate. Thus, the paramount effort is addressed to the maintenance, advocation, and high visibility of the facade. As well as bolstering one's own efforts, it is the embodiment of aspects of a grail that others may be persuaded to seek. It is the doctrine, the facade, and their subtleties, for example, shared beliefs in their validity, the rituals that preserved and cultivated them for their presentation to those who do "not yet know," that provided reassurance in the face of no demonstrable evidence for their potential successes and even in the presence of failure. It is this "true belief" in the ultimate vitality of the elements of the doctrine and facade that enables participants to speak of "next year", "when I go to——,I'll do...." and seek further for opportunities to continue their mission. From the doctrine and facade, comes the motivation to carry on beyond what real, day-to-day results seem to justify. In the instance of Kensington, after a major restructuring of ISD's organization, comments such as, "Well, we've lost a battle, but not the war," illustrate the vitality of the ideas connected with the doctrine and facade even in the face of retraction and regrouping in the realities of the school. The language of "sentiments," especially as developed by Hoffer and Klapp, has its own kind of sensational quality. Our earlier descriptive accounts should help persuade the reader that Kensington might be viewed legitimately from that perspective. An early quote from the field notes, long before Hoffer and Klapp were part of our inflectual armamentarium, adds to that credibility.

We talked at some length also about two more of his consultants, a man named Roberts and a man named Schwartz from City University. The former will be involved in curriculum and program and will be here for several days. The latter, who has interest in music education and the total curriculum, will not be coming apparently because of the financial impossibilities. Eugene spoke somewhat derogatorily of this. Apparently he thought the man should come out of the goodness of his heart or out of his own interest in the development of his own ideas in such a context at this (8/9).

What we called "goodness of his heart" and "own interest" we would phrase now as part of the morality of true belief. In our judgment, inducement-contribution theories of organization (March and Simon, 1958) have hardly touched the complexities of the attraction of personnel in innovative organizations. The principal's comments about a potential consultant clarify one aspect. Perhaps another appropriate intellectual lever is Etzioni's (1961) conception of the normative organization. Recruitment of true believers would fit this point of view.

Dimensions of True Belief

In short, sentiments, true belief, and crusading provide an initial perspective for clarifying a very important aspect of Kensington. Elaboration of this aspect of the origins of an innovative organization seems most critical Essentially we shall pursue our data and relevant theory as we seek hypotheses linking the dimensions of true belief to other aspects of the organization.

The need for remedial effort. An "image of evil" is an aspect of crusades, a noted by Klapp and others, and provides a basis for the direction of the participant's efforts. Furthermore the notion of "wrongs-to-be-rightened" provides a background for faith in the new solutions that, in turn, justifies the subsequent troubles and risk. Kensington rejected things as they were and proposed in varying degrees of detail the characteristics of a new order. In our data a great deal of the formal doctrine illustrated the wrongs and "evils" of traditional education that Kensington was to alter and replace. The superintendent's initial remarks to the staff workshop was a clarion. The content of the parent meetings incorporated the ills that Kensington was to eradicate. The building Specs chastised the discrepancy between what is taught and what is learned. The Institutional Plan's "from-to" page that redefined teacher-pupil roles, indicated clearly many of the aspects of traditional elementary education that the majority of those at Kensington wished to change. Ciosely associated with these proposals were alternations in educational process, content, materials, and building design. Thus, a part of the crusader's role is to call attention to existing "wrongs-to-be-righted" and to propose solutions for them. The data from Kensington are clear.

Total Commitment, When one commits oneself to an organization, one pledges or binds a portion of his time, energy, skills and loyalty. Typically, the organization reciprocates in the form of financial compensation, recognition, and other items valuable to an individual. By total commitment we mean and increase in time and energy beyond the formally contracted "eight hours per day" and beyond the professional knowledges and skills possesed by the staff. Satisfactions and rewards that typically come from investing time and energy in family, friends, church, clubs, community services, hobbies, and recreational pursuits are relinquished and diverted into the organization.

As we have indicated, one hypothesis we offer is that this develops, in part, as a consequence of high enthusiasm. In Kensington, the ideology surrounding the development of the fully-functioning pupil contributed to it as well. The socially integrative stance is personally expensive to actualize. At the end of the second week, the observer noted:

During our coffee break discussion, I raised the question of the norms about how much time they should be spending on school problems and how long the day would be, and how and when they would carry out the time for planning, and the like. There isn't much clarity on this, but the girls who responded indicated that they were literally working on school problems all the time. One of the schisms here is that the group with no family and no social life independent of the school, as yet, literally are involved through most of their waking existence. Most of them saw this as, over the long run, not desirable. Specifically, in terms of planning, Kay thought they might be having team meetings before school around 8:00 and curriculum and other such meetings at some time off and on during the day.

Ten days later, the observer speculated in a similar vein.

Theoretically, perhaps one of the most crucial issues that I see now lies in the degree of personal involvement that one needs to carry out the task of teaching. How much of one's life needs to be committed to the task, how much of it needs to be open, and what kinds of agreements do you need rather than some superficial methods of working together? For instance, if the roles can be spelled out bureaucratically, and if one agrees to those roles, is that the sum and substance of it and does there need to be other than minimal personal involvement beyond that? In one sense, the first week has opened all of these concerns and a number of other issues about who I am, where I am going, and the like.

However, the staff at Kensington rejected any aspects of bureaucracy, which might have delimited the range and amount of commitment or that might have formalized and specified behavioral expectations. The acceptance of egalitarianism and the eschewing of bureaucratic dimensions is not surprising in that a feeling of righteousness and of being called on to work for a higher purpose, that is, a performance beyond the requirements of ordinary duty, is a part of the sentiment structure of the crusader. As Klapp (1969) states:

"We find a great range between bureaucracy, which is lacking in the ability to intensify feelings, and violent forms of 'fun' or conflict or crusades which give a person a chance to prove himself by commitment, encounters, and ordeals".

"In general, bureaucracy has no crusading spirit".

In this sense, at Kensington there was initially little of the "alienation" or meaninglessness frequently attributed to many kinds and settings of work. Work "beyond the call of duty" was the norm.

Theoretically, the consequences of total commitment become significant at Kensington when one considers the independently developing strand of social conflict and interpersonal hostility. Among the costs and constraints of total commitment are vulnerability and risk. For although "zeal or caring beyond matter-of-fact job requirements is the beginning of a crusading spirit, fanaticism is its end point." Fanaticism implies "unreasoning zeal" and may hamper the task of evangelism, a part of the role behavior of any crusader. However, also, total commitment is a prequisite for performing as a crusader, since crusading is "called for only when the job is so difficult and extraordinary that *heroic* energies must be mobilized..." (Klapp, 1969, p. 267).The overall innovation strategy, the alternative of grandeur, opted for at Kensington was such a position and required this kind of mobilization. The tasks involved extraordinary expenditures of time, effort, creativity and loyalty.

Moreover, when one's total reward and satisfaction structure is tied to one source, failure of that source through events within or beyond one's own control and potency can have severe consequences. As hostility increased, as portions of the program failed, as administrative support changed, several faculty members were subjected to intense frustration, anxiety, severe personal debilitation, and withdrawal. At this point, again, the function of faith was illustrated, for a movement such as this needs something good enough to justify the problems, the trouble and the risk. A majority of the staff at Kensington possessed this faith in the "new elementary education." We present a summary schema of these relationships in Figure 2.1.

High aspirations. In his discussion of cooperative teaching, Shaplin (1965) attributes to teaming what seems to belong more to innovativeness and true belief.

"One of the major confusions in the team-teaching movement has been the tendency to claim all-embracing objectives and goals, on a grandiose scale, phrased in the most general terms. The goals of the team must be consistent with its size and capability".

> At Kensington, the teams were caught, to some degree, on the high aspiration and limited resources dilemma, but more basically it was the entire school that was entangled. With overtones from the various statements of the formal doctrine and with concrete efforts in the committee of the workshop area and, later, in the regular total staff meetings and, especially, in the curriculum meetings, Kensington attempted important and large alternations in American education. The extensiveness of the change, the sweeping away of the old, the implementation of the new, and a rejection of a gradualist strategy illustrate our point.

The exceedingly high aspirations that may characterize participants of a movement correspond to the specifications incorporated in the grail and, in this case, the doctrine and the facade. These high aspirations, which possibly would be deemed unrealistic by those with minimal crusading spirit, may lead to over-aggrandizement of the attempt on the part

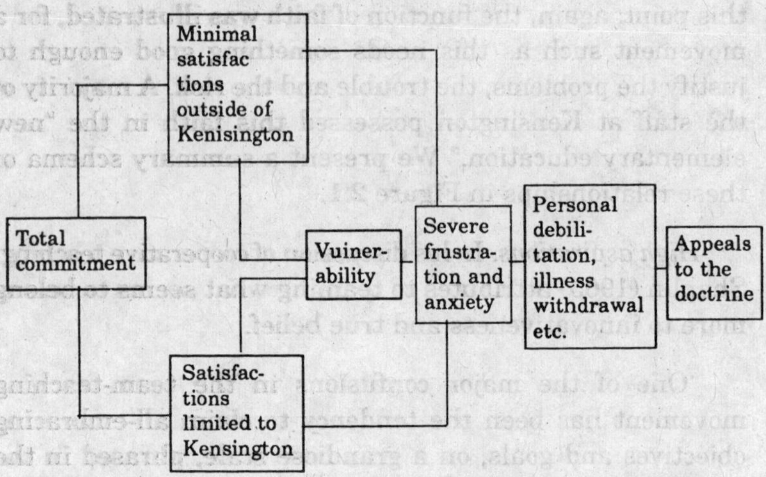

Figure 2.1. The consequences of total commitment.

of the participants in a movement that has a practical level—teaching school. This, in turn, may support fallacious assumptions about the capabilities of participants in lieu of time, ability, and work demands. As we have analyzed in our discussion of resources, the requirements for the kind of task that they attempted involved time and a specialized personnel for beyond that which is available to a school district, much less a single school, even one as well endowed as Kensington.

A framework for faith. Interestingly, Kensington, not only by being a part of a larger school system but also by design, tried to be a rational organization. But even in rational organizations there are problems that defy rationality. The selection of ultimate goals in considered by most organizational analysts to be a valuational instead of a rational process (Simon, 1957). The tremendous complexity of some educational decision requires one to settle some issues arbitrarily. At such times, it seems convenient to have agreement on "gods and bibles," that is, on who are the experts and ultimate authorities. We found this developing at several points.

On Monday morning, August 17, the principal discussed the curriculum and the overall framework. In doing this, he made explicit reference to *Planning and Organizing for Teaching,* a book by Goodlad (1963) in the National Education Association NEA "Project Instruction." The field notes report it this way:

There are several models. Bill gives a mimeo summary. Eugene thanks Bill and develops the ideas: "Model A—The function is to cover and inculcate a body of material. The organization of the school is by grades. In Model B, there is a prescribed body of knowledge by levels. There are no grades but 12 to 20 levels. It attempts to deal with individual differences by rate of progress. Model C, has a different function—learner centered, ways of knowing and thinking, a conceptual approach to learning, function of effective functioning individual. Needs a different organization; kensington follows this model. What are the implications for curriculum? What do pupils need for junior high—these books? concepts? skills? Here again I suspect we have wide differences. If junior high teacher complains the student doesn't know the solar system, I'm tempted to say I don't care. I don't think we have a prescribed body of subject matter" (8/17).

The next day the observer recorded similar data:

Another item that came up this morning in a before-school discussion concerned the kind of intellectual authority to which the teaches and the pupils in the building appeal and some notion of how this develops. So far the ASCD Yearbooks on *Knowing, Perceiving, and Becoming,* and the one on *Individualizing Instruction* are two critical volumes. Another set of volumes are the NEA reports of people like Goodlad. Today one of the books that I noticed was Berelson and Steiner's *Human Behavior,* which David was carrying with him (8/18).

As we have tried to analyze this, the heart of the issue seems to be two-fold: first, by definition, the nature of goals is an affirmation of faith, at least, at the ultimate level. Particular goals can be rationalized as means to the ultimate goals. Second, problems rapidly become very complex. This complexity is often cut through most easily by accepting the analysis made by an authority. The processes of resolution and acceptance seem facilitated by the combined influence of the principal, the district curriculum director, the Institutional Plan, and the formal doctrine.

When ideas are the primary referents, rather than existing organizations, or when there is a blending of the two, additional emphasis is focused on the selection, reading, and interpretation of written materials. In addition, the doctrine, and the published sources are sought as arbitrators of issues. Thus, in an innovative setting, emphasizing uniqueness, a great deal of faith may come to be placed in the theoretical statements of "experts" and "authorities." At Kensington both informally and in meetings, much time and effort were given to discussion and to the consideration of various ideas and positions perceived as both authoritative and applicable to the school. At this point, the extent of ideological consistency or inconsistency is highly visible.

The problems of ideological inconsistency developed early, which seems likely to happen in any new movement. Time and criticism move most positions toward consistency or toward separation into groups with more congruent belief systems. High enthusiasm in August led to the holding of beliefs that were only partially consistent. Other aspects of the doctrine contributed to the inconsistencies. In addition, there was conflict between ideas held by an individual and the ones shared by the other members of the group. The extent to which one or the other would be adhered to in the day-to-day operation of the school was also an issue. The emphasis of the training groups on individual search behavior and the team teaching's focus on cooperative behaviour and the issues of coordination and control produced ideological constraints that were never resolved. These quests and searches, whether printed or interpersonal, involve highly idiosyncratic interactions with the environment. In one sense, this too, is juxtaposed to the coordination and synchronization required by cooperative behavior. For the professional crusader, these constraints may be an onus to be avoided. In the case of one division at Kensington, the teams were dissolved and the individuals pursued their own courses. The issue seems particularly critical in education when individual development, in the context of a group setting, occurs. When reference groups are predominantly ideational and subject to differing interpretations and applications, as are most creeds, further concern develops.

Jargon. At Kensington, little was called by a usual name. Teachers were not teachers; they were academic counselors and resource specialists. Classrooms were laboratory suites, and the library was the perception core. Grade levels were gone and divisions-Basic Skills, Transition, and Independent Study-replaced them. A jargon, the technical vocabulary of a science, art, trade, sect, profession, or other special group, arose. Although, in part, necessary for the novel and unique aspects of the organization, it had a variety of additional functions.

One of the negative aspects was caught in the August field notes, as a member of the staff reflected on the new terminology:

> She feels that the entire group has been brainwashed. She likened it to the communist attempt at brain-washing people. She gave a specific instance, the failure of staff members to use certain terminology. She did not feel that one could use words such as textbook, tech, curriculum, subject matter, and other special words. She further stated that if one could say the same things only in different words it would be quite acceptable. She said, "If this isn't brainwashing, I don't know what is." She further mentioned that when she got finished with this year, there would be three words that she would never use again. These words are conceptualize, fully-functioning, and process (8/26).

Cultish aspects of jargon arose early in the program. Comments critical of traditional education appeared in labels such as "two by four" education. This is education that is restricted to the four walls of a self-contained classroom and the two covers of a textbook. As shorthand, it carried the emotional meaning of the true belief. One might argue that it foreclosed analytical thought and careful judgment.

The field notes reflect the observer's concerns in trying to view this clearly.

> The program of the school is so clouded with cliches and razzle-dazzle that it is very difficult to see clearly what will happen to the children. There will be a variety of team-teaching kinds of things going on. I can never get very much in the way of specific answers as to how this will be handled, who will be doing what, and who will coordinate them, and so on. A number of people have been hired who will be team leaders, as well as the "house coordinator," who is an experienced principal. Whether or not this will wash is a very interesting question. It is very difficult to cut through the published and dittoed materials on the program.

There seems to be a very strong assumption that the individual children after the third grade will be behaving in a way that looks to me to be very much like that of independently working college students. They will be on a variety of projects of their own choosing and of mutual choosing with the teachers. There is a strong stress on individual and independent work. I am not sure how this is going to function and what the requisite skills will be for this (12/20, pre-experimental year).

Given a combination of Kensington's novel building and organization, which reflected the creativity of a number of planners, and the sentiments of enthusiasm and true belief on the part of the staff, the role of jargon was multifaceted and had a number of implications for the participants. The jargon served as a rallying point for some of the staff, created an issue of contention for others, and provided copy for news media and contributed to the facade. For visitors and parents, it dramatized the innovative qualities and the uniqueness of the organization. On occasion, it hindered concrete thinking and the evaluation of the school and its program.

However, beyond a practical program, there are those things that the members of the movement have that outsiders do not readily see and appreciate, for example, beliefs, assumptions, sacred values, meanings, grail symbols, and the like. In the case of Kensington these attributes were the nuances of belief concerning the assumptions made in the Institutional Plan and doctrine, the interpretation and the adaptations of the writings of "authorities" and "experts," and the experiences revealed in the training groups; these elements and others were knitted together and shared via the jargon. Not only did the verbal symbols synthesize beliefs and experiences but they added to the mystique as well.

Resistance to criticism: the unassailable belief. An unassailable belief is an idea that is held so strongly and closely that it is unyielding to intellectual attack or analysis. In August, after his first interview with Shelby, the interviewer recorded a paragraph in the field notes:

> It is now 3:15 p.m. I have just spent almost four-and-one-half hours with Eugene, the Principal of the Kensington School. Summarily I might comment that our discussions moved from a general coolness and skepticism to the development of what I think is going to be quite real warmth, rapport, and ease of working together. The initial coolness centred around, I think, may skeplicism and close questioning as to how the program would work and how it would function. Eugene is very committed to the whole idea and is very excited about it. It seems as if he were jolted by the fact that someone who is to be intimately involved might really question the whole purpose and approach of the discussion. Along about the first one-third, we got this clarified in that I made a comment that I had just come out of a very traditional situation and, also, that part of my gambit was to be critical and skeptical so as to push him to speak more definitively about what he was going to do and how the building was going to function. As the discussion moved on, I began to catch some of his excitement. Also we began to find a commonality in non-schools issues on which we have some basic agreement (8/8).

Such conviction seems to create a charisma among the staff that furthers the commitment and the enthusiasm. We argue also that blind spots are created and that some issues are not though through.

Although most of the data we have drawn on in this section were obtained in August, we insert information from a May conversation with one of the staff.

His comments range back to the early part of the year and the fact that they were "hurt" by the first month over in the gymnasium in the high school. He also commented about the naivete, particularly of the ISD teachers. He was not prone to exclude himself from this naivete also. A very important point it seems to be needs to be drawn out of this in that the whole group possessed a kind of an illusion about what they were and about what they were going to do, and how it was going to happen. The older and wiser heads, such as Irma and Tom, either did not express themselves forcefully or they, too, were deluded (5/18).

The constellation of inexperience, differential influence, and unassailable beliefs seems most noteworthy. The notion of the unassailable belief helps explain an unwillingness to compromise, a part of the role of the crusader. Such unwillingness to compromise was reflected early in the year in the events surrounding the Kirkham incident. Discussions concerning his replacement became entangled in whether the new individual would be "oriented toward our goals," which was a primary reason for Kirkham's dismissal. The inclusive-exclusive dimensions of the groups' perception of themselves proved most limiting in bringing in other personnel. The underutilization of Walt Larson, the first of the long-term substitutes, as we described earlier, seemed very significant in the development of the Independent Study Division. Later David Nichols' strict adherence to the doctrine was described by erstwhile team members as "uncompromising." Interestingly, as indicated in a previous section, any vestiges of "bureaucracy," with its emphasis on structure and standardization were shunned as being inflexible. The building facilities and the program were phrased formally in terms of flexibility and adaptability. In contrast, the belief systems of some of the staff proved to be highly resistant to compromise and change.

Futuristic orientation. As Crest, the innovative psychiatric hospital (Stotland and Kobler, 1965), was spurred on by hope, enthusiasm, and the possibility of future success, thus was Kensington. The futuristic orientation that was adopted in the first few months of school continued throughout the year, although the focus changed considerably.

In retrospect, a latent function of the three-month temporary housing becomes clear. The new building became the point on which faculty sights were set and the frame of reference by which current behavior was weighed and by which it was evaluated. In some aspects the building and the anticipated influence that it was to exert grew to enlarged proportions. In part, it was not unrealistic, since the physical design was to serve as one means for adherence to the doctrine. The anticipation of the new building was a cause for hope and a renewal of enthusiasm in the face of increasing intrafaculty pressures. However, for some of the staff it was viewed as a panacea for interpersonal difficulties. Given this condition, for a time the hope expressed in the beauty and uniqueness of the building seemed to serve as a balm to lessen faculty tensions.

The noise, drudgery, and very close physical proximity of the first few months in the temporary quarters contributed to a partical esprit de corps among the staff. This enabled them to present a united facade to the parents, even when the interpersonal difficulties were greatly shaping and modifying the organizational structure, as we will present shortly in the data on the reorganization in ISD. The field notes contain some of the informal staff comments early in the fall. Shelby seemed to express faith and hope in the building as being likely to influence change in the behavior of both teachers and students. He commented that, "Some parents are expecting problems to be solved in the new building; some will be better and some worse." Yet, Jack

Davis, while in the temporary quarters, stated that, "It's hard for me to get real exited here because of the new building." Tom asked, "Do you feel things will be less acute in the new building?" And Jack replied, "Yes, a larger area, more things to do, more places to go, etc. Things should be helped with the new situation. Kids and parents are looking forward to it. There might be more room for movement. I don't know." Then Davis added, "I think they (the parents) will give us until then. They're being fair; but if nothing changes, they'll be disappointed."

In effect, hope in the future seemed to flow from inexperience in August, and from frustration in the early fall. The dimension of hope and its concomitants, as in the case of true belief, extended beyond the forays and accomplishments at Kensington. As we pointed out in the introductory epilogue, hope was finally displaced, out of the Milford District and into PS 2100, where Eugene went in February of the second year, and into the more limited individual careers and opportunities of the staff. In this way a futuristic orientation interacted with the one of faith and true belief in the ideas embodied in the "new elementary education."

Humor. Although much of our data have supported the observations of Klapp (1969), they do not confirm his concerns with humor and detachment. In delineating some of the characteristics of crusaders, he describes the crusader as taking himself seriously, lacking humor and ironic detachment toward his role, and being so utterly committed that he lacks role distance. At Kensington, beginning early in the year, humor was an integral part of the staff espirt de corps. Early humor was exemplified by "fully-functioning-Freddy," the ideal pupil product of the school. At the close of the year, a coloring-book that lampooned the attempts of the staff to make parts of the program work was developed.

It was a compendium of humor throughout the year. In this way humor, much as jargon, as we indicated previously, is a part of those characteristics the crusaders have which outsiders do not readily see nor appreciate.

Thus, humor was not absent and in most instances it grew from being able to stand back and reflect on events occurring at Kensington. In contrast to an absence of detachment and self-analysis, as suggested by Klapp, much time was devoted to verbalizing and rationalizing reasons for behavior. The cycle of questioning and explanation had its courses in both the training groups and in team teaching as a whole, which requires greater rationalization of one's intents and provides visibility of behavior. Although many of the staff were committed to the trappings of the new elementary education, they were able to employ a kind of self-consciousness to their work at Kensington and to state many of the difficulties surrounding the attempt to innvocate on a grand scale. In all of this, humor remained as a major facet of Kensington.

Inexperience, naivete, and true belief. The man on the street, the practical man, and the man of affairs, all seem to utilize a concept such as "experience" as they think about their organizations. Social scientists (for example, March and Simon, 1958; Balau and Scott, 1962), tend to make less use of it and have not engaged in intensive theoretical reduction of the concept. In the Kensington story, it loomed large. Recall our brief introduction to the staff. Of the 21 original members, seven had not taught. One of the 14 who had taught was removed before school began and replaced by an inexperienced substitute. Nine additional staff members, five aides, and four student teachers had minimal or no work experience in the public schools.

The interrelationships among enthusiasm, training, and

knowledge arose dramatically as substantive issues in pedagogy appeared during the workshop.

> Another phenomenon that has struck me is that everyone in this workshop is devoting time and attention to professional matters in a way that I, personally, have never seen in our undergraduate elementary education students or by a school faculty. In this sense, the motivation is really intense and strong, and the people are willing to devote considerable energy with the task at hand. There are some interesting aspects about this because this is done within the limitations of their ability and their training. I cringe with the notion of how much more these people ought to know about reading, how much more they ought to know about social studies methods, and how inadequate most of their training has been as they talk about it, and how crucial it might be for what they are doing. Without question, the teacher education profession, at least as I know it, is really confused. Yet, the drama of this kind of involvement is quite exciting (8/21).

Analytically, several aspects seem crucial. In part, the administrative authorities had deliberately planned the organization in this manner. They did not want old solutions to educational problems. In their own words, they believed that it would be easier to train inexperienced personnel in new approaches than to retrain experienced persons. Experience, in this usage, seems to be a broad personality variable including schema dimensions such as awareness of problems and classical solutions to problems. Additionally, we argue, it contains trait and skill dimensions in executing these solutions and a high probability of success in this execution. For instance, if a child or class is having difficulty in understanding a concept in science or social studies, classical solutions would suggest that the teacher present a relevant illustration, exercise, or book passage to be read. Besides knowing the specific illustration, content, or title, the experienced teacher would know that it was "sure fire," that it had a high probability of reaching the goal, because she had sorted these through with previous trial and error. She would have a residual set of solutions. The inexperienced teacher probably would have a less wide repertory, although this seems linked closely with a more general creativity dimension, considerably less high-probability solutions, and probably less confidence in her tactics. insofar as confidence produces cues of a self-fulfilling prophecy sort—both pupil compliance and pupil confidence of success—it becomes exceedingly important.

As we have indicated, a further aspect of teacher motivation and commitment, beyond specific confidence, is the high enthusiasm for the cause, the ideology, which we found in a greater degree in the inexperienced as opposed to the experienced teachers.

The inexperience dimension had implications for organizational structure, status, and influence early in the summer workshop. Organizational planning, skill in group discussion, and the ability for mobilization of agreement which were important in August may be considerably different from teaching. Early we hypothesized:

One other hypothesis I would offer concerns the problem that is going to face the people when they have the children thee with them. It seems to me that the individuals who are going to make out best are those who know a tremendous amount and who can make this readily available without much prior preparation. This suggests that men like Jack may be a very fundamentally important person at that time, where at this point he is not. Whether David can stand this kind of instructional pressure or whether Kay of Liz can, I don't know. Part of the question I would raise is that they have not taught and do not have the wealth of illustrations, materials, and procedures, at their fingertips that would make this very much simpler. In this sense, it's not a question of brightness, it's more a question of specific tactics and procedures.

In summary, at Kensington there was the pervasive desire for novel solutions to old educational problems. It was believed that inexperienced persons would be better able and more willing to seek and to implement new ways of going about the process of teaching. The initial sentiments of the inexperienced members of the staff were those of confidence, enthusiasm, and genuine support of the doctrine. Their commitment and willingness to invest great amounts of effort in the program exemplified their true belief in the tenets of the movement. However, in the practical aspects of the enterprise, the inexperienced persons had limited skills in teaching, little knowledge of "sure fire" techniques applicable to the classroom, and minimal awareness of the wide range of problems that may accompany the day-to-day activities of teaching. All of these point to the low level of information characteristic of many of the participants. Although the ideational qualities of the mandate "Go build a school" were mastered, the information input about the practical aspects was limited.

At the level of application, these factors interacted to produce problems in the classroom and eroded some of the original confidence and enthusiasm; frustration, anxiety, and dicouragement increased. However, through the most dismaying times at the practical level, the field notes taken at the team meetings, the curriculum meetings, and of informal contacts indicate continued faith in the ultimate principles of the doctrine. This illustrates the resilience of inexperience and buoyancy of the true believer. Likely the most stringent trial of a novice crusader is survival of the often impairing blows of experience. The professional true believer has triumphed!

Although Klapp does not speak specifically of inexperience he points to "an inherent naivete in crusading, so that at a certain point in sophistication people might find it impossible to believe that they could restore their identities or their society by such means" (1969, p. 310). Partial understanding and highly-bounded rationality may be requisites for participation in a crusade. Hoffer suggests "ignorance of the difficulties" entailed in change as a characteristic of participants. At another point in time, with more experience, information, and sophistication, the naivete of inexperience might diminish and might preclude the attempt to provide individualized programs for 200 children in a gymnasium, write curricula and prepare materials for all curricular areas for K through 6, reject textbooks, and master team teaching, all in the space of nine months.

Conclusion. Hoffer (1951) ties together several aspects of sentiment in an organization as he describes facets of the *True Believer,* the man of fanatical faith who is ready to sacrifice his life for a holy cause:

> "For men to plunge headlong into an undertaking of vast change, they must be intensely discontented yet not destitute, and they must have the feeling that by the possession of some potent doctrine, infallible leader or some new technique, they have access to a course of irresistible power. They must also have an extravagant conception of the prospects and potentialities of the future. Finally, they must be wholly ignorant of the difficulties involved in their vast undertaking. Experience is a handicap" (p. 20).

In the judgment of our case, his account underemphasises the positive attraction of healthy people trying to make a better world. True believers come for many reasons. Some seem to have a relatively simple faith in working toward educational ideals that they hold sincerely and uncomplicatedly. Others perceive, quite clearly and consciously, the possibilities of combining their faith and their careers. Others seem to be searching for identity and a positive self-concept, as Klapp suggests. Although Kensington had those who were "intensely discontented" and "those who crave to be rid of an unwanted self," the majority were finding as freedom and an opportunity to create that is usually not available in the public schools—either from administrative fiat or from informal faculty "understandings." In addition, innovative organizations will have serious continuity problems because the staff will go on new quests. This departure is due, in part, to their high visibility and to being "bought" or competed for, combined with the commitment to advance the tenants of the movement. The grail is elusive; the quest is eternal. As shown earlier, Hoffer's analysis of potent doctrine, infallible leader, new techniques, extravagant conceptions of the future, ignorance of the difficulties, and the role of inexperience have a telling validity. He who would engage in large-scale innovative programs must be cognizant of the role of true belief that is endemic to the process.

The Broader Implications of True Belief

Broadening and Continuing the Crusade. The sentiment of intense commitment to the "rightness" of the cause enables participants to go forth with a sense of mission. Klapp observes that there is a "determination to go ahead in spite of lack of public support, even with public opposition." This was amply illustrated by the data from Kensington. We discuss in other sections of the book the various publics of an organization. Although Kensington was considered by some of the district officials initially as a protected subculture, it was less and less protected as time passed. A mission to say something about the "new elementary education" both locally and nationally was undertaken. Public opposition was evident, both among professionals and parents. However, for the crusader with true belief in the cause, this enhances the responsibility to fight an evil that others do not perceive. That one has discovered and is assailing that which is not perceived as injurious by others is further testament to the need for the movement. In this way, responses of opposition and apathy from one's public may be viewed as reinforcement for the mission. Thus, for those who truly believe, failure conceived as opposition or lack of support from one's publics and constituents is unknown, it only serves to legitimate the tasks of evangelism.

Socialization, visability and mobility. Our data illustrate well how a movement such as Kensington was a part of what may be viewed as providing a form of socialization for the neophyte crusader. Reference to some early notes indicates how involvement at Kensington was viewed as a preparatory training for innovative tasks yet to come:

This has been a very full day and it is difficult to get all the details in that one must. One of the kinds of things that seems to me to be most relevant is trying to state initially why people have come to the Kenisington School. The general motives and goals became more and more explicit as the day wore on. For instance, Tom is working in the curriculum and instruction area and has about completed a doctorate. He has several years experience as a teacher, as a visiting teacher, and as a school principal. Actually five years in the latter. This kind of experience in the Kensington School as the key man in the Perception Core area will give him a very unique experience that will enable him to move to almost any teacher's college curriculum and instruction department in the country. And probably with a very good salary and with a very unique position. Almost the exact same thing can be said for the "other administrator" in our small group, Bill. He's on the make, and he wants to move ultimately into a college curriculum position. He is working on his doctorate at State University. Running through the entire group, including these two people, is some desire to get finally into a position where they could carry out teaching operations in line with the kinds of theory and preaching they have been doing. This, when the kids come into the building, should make a very interesting day of reckoning for some of them. One or two look more like individuals who are trying to solve their own personal problems. Wanda and Jean look like individuals who have taught a while, although in Jean's case just a few years, and are interested in being able to implement some of the things that they were not able to do in the other building. Another seems more like a hostile subject matter specialist who is going to show all of the stupid education professors just how it should have been done. Kay apparently had a very enjoyable, exciting experience in her internship and seemingly wants to elaborate and to build on this (8/10).

Later the same day, I chatted a few minutes about a number of things with Bill. He raised the problem that I might he interested in the personal goals of the people on the staff. Alec and John were around at the time. In effect, he was saying that many of the people were using the school as a jumping-off place for later things. He argues that this determines some of the things, for example, makes a difference, in what he does, because he will ultimately move on from here. It is interesting that I had been raising the same nation in my notes this morning. He came from a position of principal, which is hard for a number of people to understand. Alec reported some Welcome Wagon person making such comments to his wife. John raised the same kind of notion that many of his friends from Ohio were skeptical as to why he would be coming here in that he has finished all of this course work for his doctorate and also has had a couple of years college teaching experience (8/10).

"From the ... view of the recruit, the crusade is a role opportunity: to form oneself according to a pattern not ordinarily available, to rise to a higher level of input (commitment) and output (heroism), to test oneself by mortal encounter and engagement; above all, then, to find a new conception of oneself" (Klapp, 1969 p. 269).

The unique role opportunities were available, and exceedingly high inputs and engagement were requisites. As shown in the notes, commitment was to the movement for the new elementary education, and Kensington was an important but temporary training ground, a step for many of the staff as they searched to create careers as professional innovators. Commitment was to issues and ideas as well as to anything as place-bound as the generation of social structure of a beginning, fledgling organization. The ideas were portable, applicable elsewhere, and the educational world was waiting, as exemplified by the many visiting educators, the written inquiries, and the coverage by the media both in educational and popular publications.

In a more general sense, this fits the notion that not the "destination but the journey is important; though you do not get there, you may have experienced something along the way that is significant" (Klapp, p. 293).

The emphasis on the processual instead of on the substantive which was prevalent at Kenisngton merged well with the career intentions of the staff, their belief systems, and the means taken by some to find new identities. Thus, a participant may experience and may refine his expertise as a proponent of a movement. Indeed, part of one's role is to become a better crusader for something that extends beyond the framework of any one institution of the "Bataan Phenomenon" and the esteem accorded to Shelby, who was moving to a new position to carry out further aspects of the ideology, well illustrates the point.

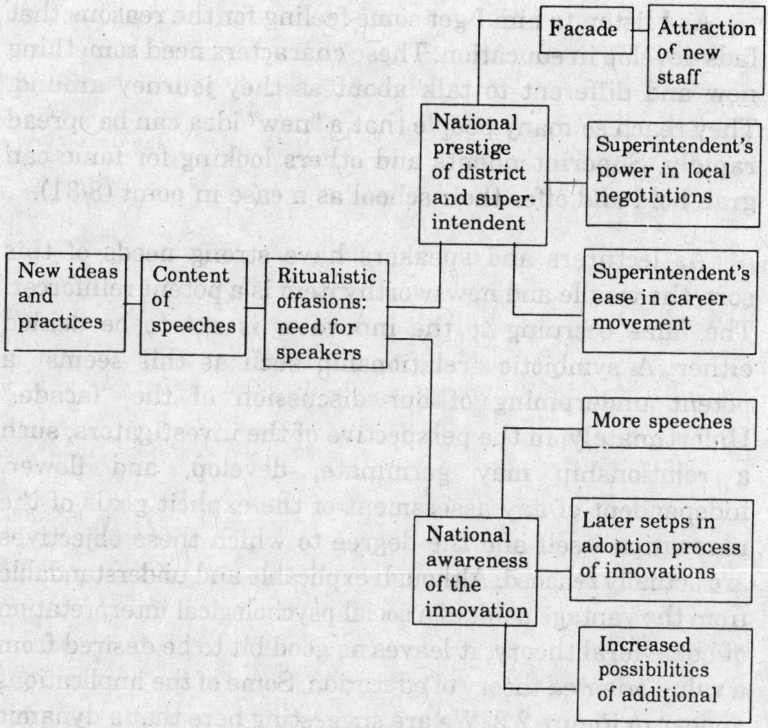

Figure 2.2. The dynamics of educational innovation in the context of true belief.

Beyond milford. During the August teachers meeting , the Milford School District followed the standard ritual of having a program with an out-of-town speaker who trades glowing epithet with the superintendent. Spanman introduced the speaker as an educational statsmen of "Ideas and integrity." The speaker, in turn, lauded the superintendent and the bright spots of Milford. He talked of the significance of teaching, "a job to build a dream on." The observer, who had attended opening night and had seen the play before, suggested an hypothesis which, although a bit cynical, still extends the conceptualization of issues in true belief and innovation.

As I listen to him I get some feeling for the reasons that fads develop in education. These characters need something new and different to talk about as they journey around. They reach so many people that a "new" idea can be spread rapidly. Superintendents and others looking for fame can grab hold and offer their school as a case in point (8/31).

As lecturers and speakers have strong needs of this sort, the visible and newsworthy item is a potent reinforcer. The fame occruing to the innovator is not to be denied either. A symbiotic relationship such as this seems a potent underpining of our discussion of the "facade." Unfortunately, in the perspective of the investigators, such a relationship may germinate, develop, and flower, independent of any assessment of the explicit goals of the innovation itself and the degree to which these objectives are actually reached. Although explicable and understandable from the vantage point of a social psychological interpretation of behavioral theory, it leaves as good bit to be desired from a value-oriented theory of education. Some of the implications appear in Figure 2.2. We are suggesting here that a dynamic exists external to the main arena, the school itself, and that part of the nature of "the broader content of true belief" lies in these outside persons who are caught up in their own system of psychological forces and, as a consequence, help create, extend, and perpetuate innovations such as Kensington.

Conclusion

A general theory of the building of an institutional core in an innovative organization remains a major unfinished task from our analysis of Kensington. Interdependencies exist among (1) schools as a particular kind of organization, (2) innovative schools as a special organizational subcase, (3) self-selection to innovative schools of persons characterized by a quality of true belief, (4) the emotional qualities inherent in a socialization procedure such as T-groups, and (5) the broader context of innovation in the national educational Zeitgeist. Our data and analysis would suggest that educational administrators, parents, and interested citizens cannot ignore these issues as they try to improve public education in the abstract case and individual public schools in the particular case.

Selection of a Social Base

The organization's relationship to its environment precedes, or at least provides, a context for the building of an institutional core that in turn precedes, or provides, a context for formalization. We have spoken of Kensington's problems in formalization and of its strategies, tactics, and problems in building an institutional core. Briefly we now consider Kensington's relationship to its environment.

"On Being out Front"; an Initial Description and Conceptualization of the Social Base

There is an old story which suggests that the leader of a parade should be out in front of the marching bands and the other members of his entourage. However, if he gets too far in front, he no longer leads the parade; the group may well be following someone else. This seems particularly applicable to the problems of an innovative school and its general leadership. We caught a taste of this in the early field notes.

I also heard about the in-group or ruling clique or "club," as it is called, which exists in the school system. Essentially this is Spanman, Eugene and Jerl. It also will include most of the Kensington staff ultimately. There may be one or two others. In a system with, at least, one high school and two junior highs and nine elementary schools this an awfully small core, it seems to me at this point. It raises some question about the stability of the whole enterprise. It also raises some question in my own mind about an elitist conception of leadership. They are way out ahead of their school district, of their staff, and of the community. The balance between how much ahead of the parade and how much their strength derives from the group that one leads in open to real question here. Some of this came up at another point in the evening as both Jerl and Eugene made comments about the degree to which the community is informed about what is going on. Apparently there are a number of half-truths circulating about the nature of the school. Essentially these are omission errors rather than commission errors. For instance, they talked some about the ungraded aspect of the school but talked very little about the almost total permissiveness of the curriculum in social studies and in science. They feel the parents would not understand what they are trying to do. Apparently they have talked among themselves a good bit about how much should be communicated to the parents before the actual operation and opening of the school (8/9).

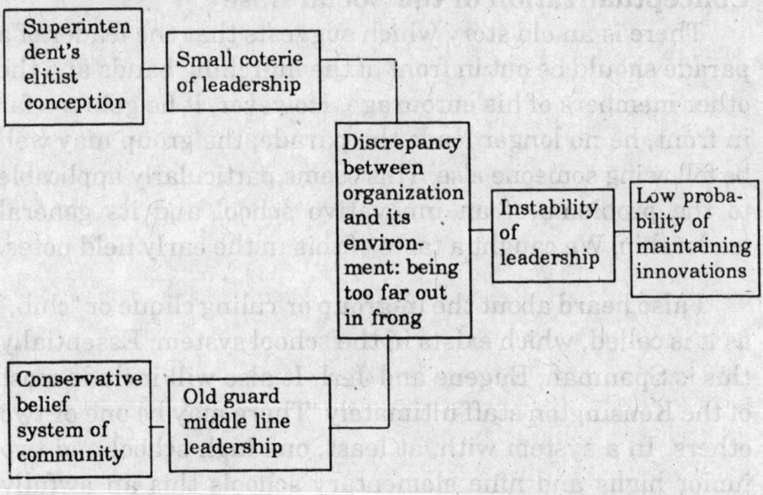

Figure 2.3. The issues in an innovative organization's social base.

In short, we were raising hypotheses concerning aspects of what Selznick would call the "social base." The educational leadership seemed seemed a part from the district patrons. The core of the leadership seemed small relative to the size of the school organization. The district seemed only partially aware of the changes underway in general in Milford and at Kensington in particular. All this seems to have significance for the probabilities that innovation will be maintained. Figures 2.3 summarizes these hypotheses.

The Multiple Facets of the Environment

At a very concrete level, one of the most striking generalizations is that the social environment has a number of discriminable parts. Each of these parts is a miniature social system in itself. These systems have interdependencies among themselves as well as with Kensington. In our case, the central office of the Milford Schools, the group of elementary principals, the school board, the district patrons, and the Kensington patrons had significant influence on the school. As we discuss the facade, the relevant publics, as parts of the social environment, expand to include the local, state, and national educational establishments as well as the national audience that reads the mass media.

The divided central office. Although evidence of district-wide problems occurred all year and in many forms, we viewed them dramatically in December.

Eugene told of conflict between himself and Howard from the central office. The latter wants to have more to do with the 'building than Eugene wants him to have. There have been a whole series of incidents. Last summer Eugene happened to be around when the order went out for the chairs in the school. He ordered three sizes and Howard had wanted to order six sizes. It was not clear to me whose decision it really was and apparently it's not clear generally. Eugene made a comment that Steven had changed some over the course of the last six months since August. When I asked him to pin down the change, he mentioned that he was turning many things over to Howard, Adolph, and Calvin, As I see it, the essence of this is that the superintendent is working through the formal, established channels and, also, may be trying to tighten the total ship in terms of the community problems that he has. For Eugene, this means that the superintendent rides the fence on issues instead of giving him total support for whatever he wants to do. This may mean that there is some equivocation and the two may not be seeing things so congruently any more. Other points of conflict between Howard and Eugene lie in the size of the chairs that will be out in the perception core. Eugene wants them all the same size because the tables are all the same height and Howard wants them of different heights. When I asked Eugene who officially had responsibility for the building and, in effect, when the keys were turned over, he didn't have a clear answer. He made a guess that it was supposed to be his last July when he became principal of the building. The feeling I have is that this is another area in which Steven has not only not been clear in operating through channels but has been vacillating back and forth, and that nobody really knows who is responsible for what. Another area of conflict has occurred, since the plans were officially set, and Howard's committee was dissolved, and the more recent evolution of changes in the building. In effect, we have two people for whom the school is "their baby." The system seems rife with conflict.

These points suggest once again that one of the necessary subsequent studies is to look carefully at the total district and the impact that this has on the particular school building. This general confusion that appears to exist at the district level seems to be transmitted right on down into the Kensington School. Another case in point of the district influence on the school, and what may be some very negative consequences in terms of the program, is the fact that Howard pushed for the move to the new building to come early.

According to on comment, and I heard it one at least one other occasion, Howard had promised the building would be ready by Thanksgiving, and he was caught wanting to maintain this and to maintain his position with the school board. The pressure was more personal in this sense rather than the need for the junior high facilities. If this is the case, and if it could have been made open and honest, then they could have moved one of the other divisions first and could have gotten it settled in that fashion. But when he had to take the rationalization, if it be a rationalization, of the junior high space problem, then it sewed up a whole series of other events that now have come about in a very dramatic and unhappy order.

Another illustration of the lack of clarity in the system generally and in the impact of the district on the building concerns the fact that Jack perceives his role as science consultant in the district as being more significant than Eugene views it. Eugene says that the district work should be supplementary to total responsibility to the building. Which days Jack is released depends really on Eugene's beneficence. What it does, though, is to put the people in ambiguous spots in that Jack has to keep asking for favors, which is always a dangerous phenomenon, instead of having the right or his due in terms of having days off to work on the district material. As we talked about the flavor of this, it is quite different from what occurred early in the year. As it stands now, this is a recurring problem (12/10).

In effect, these and other decisions concerning materials, supplies and money had a pronounced impact on the growth and development of Kensingtaon. Particularly, they seem to relate to the early conception of the school as a protected subculture and to the present reality; perceptions of what Kensington was and should be varied greatly among the district officials. These divergences, coupled with the ones internal to the staff, proved to be difficult taskmasters for the beginning organization.

The elementary principals. In most school districts that we have come to know well, we have been struck by the potency of the group of elementary school principals. In general, they seem to form an important reference group for the individual principal. The principal's decisions regarding his building seem to be conditioned by the impact of this group, as well as his own building staff. His evaluation of the success of his building program seems to be set by the norms of this group of principal colleagues. To the best of our knowledge, little systematic theoretical analysis or empirical data are available on these colleaguial cliques of principals. In the Milford District such a group of peers existed; however, Shelby was not a part of it. They were of the "old guard," and they viewed him as a deviant newcomer.

A lack of relationship with a group of this kind means one is not part of the informal informational grapevine. Also one does not have a group of equals involved in essentially the same set of problems, for instance, administering a building, with whom to turn for the informal give and take of advice and relevant perspectives. Also, in most district the principals have a strong policy-making function, since they have the intimate contacts with the community through the parents and they are prime channels for the flow of information up the hierarchy to the central decision-makers. Similarly, they are the key line offices for implementing the flow of policy decisions and commands from the superintendent and his central staff. Although we have little data on these issues, our impressions were that a minimization of these forces occurred early in the year and that there was an increasing strength of these forces later in the year. A careful description and analysis of the dynamics of this would have been an important supplement to our present discussion. Also, in subsequent years the intended diffusion process of Kensington's innovations to the other schools would have been fascinating if our tentative analysis of Shelby's relationship to the others is substantially correct.

The interdependence of Shelby and the other elementary principals, and the involvement of a high-ranking central office administrator, Jerl Cohen, appears in the field notes.

Another interesting phenomenon to this point is the fact that, although we are concerned with the one building, Kensington, by focusing at this level one gets involved immediately in the interrelationship with other buildings and with the broader part of the system. The sequence that is important here concerns moving from an understanding of the classroom and the need to go outside of it to the total building to gain a perspective. Now when we are at the building level the interlocking between other buildings becomes very critical. In this regard, part of the discussion centered on the impact that Jerl Cohen's presence might have on the rest of the system. If he spends this much time with the Kensington School, then that would the other eight principals think about their relative status and their relative needs. Both Eugene and Jerl are sensitive to this. The problem is a very fascinating one of looking at the same sets of issues from the vantage points of people who are placed in different positions within the system. Small wonder that there often is confusion and misunderstanding among people in different spatial and hierarchical positions.

The Kensington patrons. At a number of points we have indicated aspects of the relationship between Kensington and its patrons, another part of Kensington's environment. Although the nuances were intriguing and fascinating, the story is too long to be presented here. The major subgroups we would accent are: (1) a small loyal group who worked with the school throughout the year to help translate the ideals into day-to-day practices; (2) another small group who were opposed to the ideals in the doctrine and its correlated practices and who tried to get the school to look like their image of a more traditional elementary school; and (3) a large group of patrons who knew very little about the school and what was happening in its program. Much of the parental involvement occurred in the patrons organization and in open staff-patron meetings at the school.

The Kensington program intended close working relationships between home and school. On Wednesday, September 16, during the second week of school, an open house was held for the ISD parents. The notes, dictated late that evening, clarify additional aspects of Kensington.

I have come from a long parent-teachers meeting at the Kensington School. As I listened to the program develop, it seemed to me, logically, that one way of organizing the notes would be to list and comment on the questions that were asked. As the evening wore on, I also had a number of more generalized effective as well as cognitive responses. For instance, I had the very strong impression that the parents were asking quite specific, quite pertinent, and quite thorny questions. It seemed to me that almost universally they were right on the point. Second, I had the feeling that the parents, although they varied in the degree of hostility and support they had toward the program, were very sincere and very concerned about their children. Third, I kept wondering what educational psychology as a science of behavior had to say to these teachers and to these parents.

More specifically then to the notes on the questions that were being asked. First, one man asked: How do the teachers know what the individual children are doing? He raised it in the context of Alec's math program in which Alec had 200 students. He just did not see how it could be possible in those conditions. Alec's answer here, it seems, was caught on the program of a week ago, the program this week, and the ideal program. Nowhere did he or anyone else make clear the fact that these were three different kinds of programs and some of them could not be defended easily. The questions could not be answered and the issues defended on one aspect where they could on another. Second, one woman asked why they had physical education (PE) everyday even though they have the short program. As far as I know, the staff had not thought about the educational soundness of PE in the shortened program. The PE program seemed like a very reasonable and possible alternative and, as it is set up now, basically it gives every teacher a free period in which to do other work and to have a cup of coffee. Although it would involve some messy scheduling problems, it also suggests the very viable way to alter the program to get more instructional time or T-group-type time into the program. Third, there was a question raised about how the children make up the time that's lost in the T-groups. No one, however, asked whether the T-group was a wise idea or not. Fourth, a parent asked about the spelling program and when the children would get specific instruction in this. This typically was handled by both Irma and Eugene in terms of the words the kids actually used and of learning how to spell them. Fifth, the question was raised of communicating with parents about the child's difficulties and the procedure for this. Here the parent-conference answer was not wholly viable because the teachers each have 200 kids and they cannot have 200 conferences. In this also, it seems that the alteration of the program to its current status left many aspects undefendable in the same way that last week's part of the program left many aspects undefendable. For instance, conferences would be the academic counselor's job, yet now they do not have academic counselors. The staff was hooked on all kinds of ifs, and buts, and ands. Sixth, the question was raised about that happens to the kids of these two years, or however long, turn into out to be a failure. Here, again, the risk aspect was just not faced up to. Seventh, the question was raised about what would happen to the kids if they went into junior high school this next year. This got everybody involved in a discussion about the rumors that the whole system was moving toward the Kensington-type program. When Eugene indicated this, he immediately was faced with the question of how fast and when and what would happen at Hillside Elementary School next year. He apparently had left in open-ended as to when they would have it done, and one man's daughter was very conscientious and did not know whether she should have it all done by tomorrow or whether it should take a longer period of time. The father was very upset about this lack of clarity. There was a question raised also about the kids who were put off into the special section, and the possible repercussions of this. This is an interesting one in that little consideration was given to what the children thought or what the other children thought. (My personal guess would be, and it's rather a superficial one, that there has been no much hubbub and shifting and changing around that there is little or no discrimination by the children toward each other on the basis of anything of this kind. In that sense, when everything is confused and from the children's point of view, I suppose, quite disorganized, it's impossible to feel that you are being discriminated against. You never know for sure just exactly what's happening to anybody else).

There was also in the group considerable support for the school. Some of this was of a backhanded sort in that one couple commented about how unhappy they have been with St. Mary's School which has had a new much program every year for the last three years, and about which their daughter was terribly confused. Others, obviously, were caught by the excitement of the possibilities of the program and were urging "patience," "let's see", and "give them more than a week and a half". Blended into this were comments indicating the very strong aspirations many of these parents have for the children. For instance, many of the parents want their children to have advantages that they did not have. They want them to compensate for mistakes they feel were made in their own educational program. They want them to be able to accomplish things that they themselves have not accomplished. Related to this also, it seemed to me, were problems that the parents were having with their children or problems that the kids had in the school or in other schools. This was perhaps best typified by the man who carried the brunt of the dissatisfaction. He has a son in junior high school who apparently is a real goof off and will not do a damn thing. He also has a daughter who is overly conscientious and a concerned that everything be right. He's mad at the Milford Junior High School and their program; he's mad at Kensington and their program and, my guess would be, he will be unhappy all along the line no matter what happened to his children insofar as it did not shift them from these two extreme sorts of responses (9/16).

The school was involved intimately with the parents. At the evening meetings difficult questions were raised. Although a few parents seemed to be displacing their hostility on a convenient target, most seemed to have a picture of the public school as a vehicle for the better life that they wanted for their children. They wanted to be sure that the new program would facilitate this major goal.

In the local metropolitan area, the Milford District has had a history and a reputation of conflict. The prior superintendent came and went out of the picture several times before Spanman was selected. The district had grown several times over in size in the last decade. The new arrivals, lower-middle-class whites, wanted better homes and better schools than they thought they could obtain in the nearby central city, which was becoming rapidly a black ghetto.

They projected aspirations for their children that seemed, at times, to be higher than the district-wide ability tests and the family socioeconomic status indicated were feasible. However, our data here were too limited to suggest very intensive analyses and generalizations.

The nonunanimous board. Although we attended only a few meetings of the school board, the observations were supplemented with conversations and with observations of board members on their occasions. Uniformly, the majority decisions supported the Spanman administration. Uniformily, there was minority opposition in verbal exchanges, if not in voting. Late in the year as rumors as well as an actuality of Spanman's leave of absence for the coming year occurred, the board began to have significant impact on Kensington. For instance, the Milford principals' freedom to allocate funds for teacher aides instead of for certified teachers was disallowed. Late in the year, Kensington suffered heavily from this controversy. In short, the board was split over the grand design for Milford and split over the specific program at Kensington. As such, it illustrates well another face of the multiple facets of Kensington's environment.

Alternative Conceptualization's of the Environment

Our data, as we have reported them from the field notes, suggest that further conceptualization of the organization's environment must be made if we are to clarify the nature of Selznick's social base problem in the origins of innovative organizations. Dill (1962) raises two broader metatheoretical stances for carrying out such an analysis:

"Most of the work of developing an adequate theory of environmental influences on organizational behavior lies ahead. Considerable work is now being done, and two directions of study seem particularly promising. One is an attempt to dimensionalize variables of human personality and intelligence. This requires considerable faith in the adequacy of such techniques as factor analysis and the linearly independent dimensions that such techniques generate to represent significant influences on other variables that we want to study. Such faith abounds, though; and some imaginative steps have been taken...

The second direction of investigation is more consistent with the approach that I have suggested here. This is the effort to conceptualize individuals or organizations as information processing systems and then to simulate, usually with the aid of electronic computers and related 'hardware', the environment to which they are exposed.. The trick in building a model of the environment under such circumstances is not in isolating characteristic factors or dimensions, but in writing programs and setting up systems to generate and to present information to an individual or an organization in the same manner that the 'real world' (pp. 107,109).

In part, the kind of theoretical stance one takes depends on the kinds of questions one hopes to answer or the kind of problems one hopes to solve.

Dimensional analysis. Dimensional analysis helps one see the structure of the environment. For instance, as we described the multiple facets of Kensington's environment we might argue that the latent dimension is one of complexity, that is heterogeneous (high complexity) to homogeneous (low complexity). A highly complex environment probably entails the development of multiple goals, multiple activities, and multiple faces and facades. This suggests, too, the possibility that consistency and formalization in an organization will be difficult to achieve and that leadership and resources will have to be allocated here. In short, we are arguing that relationships will exist between such an environmental condition and each of the variables contained within one's conception of the organization.

We suggest several further dimensions that seemed latent in the field notes. The supportive-non-supportive variables interacts with the complexity dimension. Some parts of the environment, the superintendent, were strongly supportive while other parts, for instance the divided central office, were less supportive. The environment was not stable. As the year wore on Kensington's environment changed. The departure of the superintendent had a major impact on the school. This changing administrative structure illustrates also the issue of potency and involvement of the environment or, at least, part of it. Members of the divided central office were differentially involved and, particularly with the superintendent's departure, they became much more potent elements on the environment.

The environment as information. Most of our analysis of the "environment-as-information" model occurs in a later chapter in which we deal with the administration of Kensington. At this moment, we would stress several essential but often latent aspects of this point of view.

In the environment-as-information position there is an irrevocable tie with a time dimension. At time one (T_1) the environment presents itself to the organization. The organization processes the information and then acts at time two (T_2). Meanwhile, the environment changes through its dynamics, insofar as it is composed of organizations and individuals, and changes also because of its scanning of organizational action at time two. Consequently, the environment may be different at time three when the organization scans again. The handling of processes, changes over time, is an important and difficult methodological, theoretical and practical problem.

Implicit also in this conception is the phenomenon of social exchange. The organization requires resources in which to carry out its work to reach its goals. A business organization exchanges products or outputs for money which it exchanges in turn for further inputs. A school district through its board and superintendent provides an education to the pupils of the geographical area and, in turn, receives financial, resources for hiring teachers, buying books, maintaining buildings, and so forth. An individual school, such as Kensington, competes with the other schools of the district for supplies, equipment, teachers, aides\ and other resources. Each school provides intermediary services in terms of organization and program and terminal services in instructing pupils. These outputs are exchanged for some portion of the general resources. In effect, the goals of the organization are set in terms of the needs of the environment, that is, for what the environment is willing to exchange its outputs. These environmental outputs become resources for the organization. As we discuss later, Kensington was a "protected subculture", which meant that special rules governed the exchange between the school and its environment.

Thompson (1967) develops several concepts to enhance the environment-as-information analysis. Domain refers to what the organization will or will not do in relationship with the interacting parts of its environment. As a general rubric, it locates the organization within its environment and in terms of inputs and outputs. Domain consensus is the common view of the organization as held by the relevant others who compose the environment.

At Kensington, the most important element of the environment was the superintendent, Steven Spanman, and his immediate deputy, Jerl Cohen. Shelby was their intimate colleague and associate. The mandate, which we described previously, was the most significant item of information in Kensington's environment It stated the initial terms of Kensington's existence both as a support and as an outline for goals and organizational structure. The Institutional

Plan was Shelby's response to the mandate. In turn, this response became a stimulus and a guide to the later action, processes, and structure of Kensington. It led to recruitment and socialization procedures, that is, forming the institutional core. Indirectly, the mandate and Institutional Plan contributed, along with the developing institutional core, to both formalization and to the problems in formalization of Kensington's organizational structure.

Summary

The origins of a developing and changing organization are most interesting phenomena to observe. The problems of selecting a social base, building an institutional core, and formalizing procedures were issues that faced Kensington as a beginning organization. In a very brief statement, which we discovered long after we had made our observations and developed our analyses, we found Stinchcombe (1965) discussing the "liability of newsness." He says:

"... there are poorly understood conditions that affect the comparative death rates of new and old organizations. As a general rule, a higher proportion of new organizations fail than old. This is particularly true of new organizational *forms*, so that *if an alternative requires new organization,* it has to be much more beneficial than the old before the flow of benefits compensates for the relative weakness of the newer social structure".

His analysis, suggests four major factors that are appropriate as summary generalization for our data:

"(a) New organizations, especially new types of organizations, generally involve new roles, which have to be learned".

Our notes and analysis, not only in this chapter but throughout the book, reiterate in a multitude of concrete ways the truth of this principle.

"(b) The process of inventing new roles, the determination of their mutual relations and of structuring the field of rewards and sanctions so as to get maximum performance, have high costs in time, worry, conflict, and temporary inefficiency".

Time and energy appear and reappear as underestimated expenditures of limited resources. Similarly, anxiety, conflict, and difficulties in goal attainment were rampant.

"(c) New organizations must rely heavily on social relations among strangers. This means that relations of trust are much more precarious in new than old organizations...".

Kensington developed and used a number of procedures in recruiting and socializing to help cope with this problem, but it remained an issue. Further aspects are raised both explicitly and implicitly in a later chapter as we discuss "Dilemmas in Democratic Administration."

"(d) One of the main resources of old organizations is a set of stable ties to those who use organizational services".

The linkages with the environment of parents, central office personnel, and other schools in the district, we have observed to be multiple and often conflicting. Some of them were deliberate and part of the innovative strategy, and some were unintended consequences of new organizational structures.

In short, we are arguing that Conceptualizing Organizational Origins and Development is a case study in the "liability of newness." As a single case, Kensington had a number of idiosyncratic aspects that gave a subtlety and vividness to the phenomena. The resources, the multifaceted environment, and the absence of a social structure are ways of talking about the same issues. At this point we encourage the reader to return to the descriptive chapters in which we narrated briefly the origin, development, and change at Kensington.

"Building the institutional core" is the second task suggested by Selznick. Creating an initially homogeneous staff has a variety of consequences:

"(1) . . . indoctrinate newcomers along desired lines. (2) . . . provide assurance that decision-making will conform, in spite as well as letter, to policies that may have to be formulated abstractly or vaguely. (3) The development of derivative policies and detailed application of general rules will thus be guided by a shared general perspective"..

Selznick argues that selective recruiting and shared experiences provide twin procedures for handling the problem. In regard to these issues, he makes generalizations that our data suggest must be sharply limited or qualified.

"The creation of an institutional core is partly a matter of selective recruiting. . . . By choosing key personnel from a particular social group, the earlier conditioning of the individuals becomes a valuable resource for the new organization".

In a new organization that is an innovative one, the criteria for selection are considerably more ambiguous, since the nature of the desired earlier learning is not clear. The option of accenting highly recommended but inexperienced teachers and the aspiration to train them in the new directions seems, in hindsight, to have resulted in a host of consequences, many of which were dysfunctional for Kensington. Also, as we talk to the true belief in an innovative organization, important self-selective personality factors seem to operate in terms of availability for recruitment to an innovative setting.

Selznick's further generalizations regarding the building of an institutional core are interesting in the light of the data from Kensington.

"But core building involves more than selective recruiting. Indoctrination and the sharing of key experiences—especially internal conflicts and other crises—will help to create a unified group and give the organization a special identity".

Indoctrination, or socialization, occurred in the summer workshop. The T-groups, the division, team, and committee meetings, and the Institutional Plan and contributed toward the imbuing of principles and doctrines. Interwoven and extending into and throughout the year, internal conflicts and crises occurred. They did give Kensington a special identity, but they did not create a unity. Our guess would be that for unity to be achieved an organization must be successful in the eyes of the participants and in the eyes of significant others. That is the sine qua non. If one has that, the internal conflicts and crises provide stimuli for high emotion that has a positive, exciting quality to it, and such sentiments then can lead to unity and identity. Our observations of the "Bataan phenomenon" in the introductory epilogue suggest additional intricacies and qualifications to Selznick's more general statement.

When he speaks of "formalization," the third developmental problem, Selznick comments:

> "The organization reduces its dependence on the personal attributes of the participants by making supervision more routine and by externalizing discipline and incentive".

Implicit in his statement is a concern for When? and Where? and How soon? Formalization is attained within the organization. The gains from early formalization are clarity in communication and command. The losses are limitations in flexibility, open-endedness, and freedom for leadership decisions. Kenington presented several unique twists regarding formalization. First, a high degree of formalization existed early in the manifestation of the formal doctrine known as the Institutional Plan. As we argued elsewhere, formalization of this kind may have come too early. Second, the doctrine itself accented flexibility as an important subgoal. Third, a variety of experiences, for example, the T-groups, accented a lack of formalization in interpersonal relationships. Fourth, Shelby exhibited contrasting leadership modes of total non-directiveness to unswerving commitment to elements in the Institutional Plan. Fifth, styles of the staff varied from almost total personal autonomy to high willingness to accept organizational or subgroup perspectives. In short, formalization was not of a single piece at Kensington, and the consequences were multiple as well. The economy of formalization of social structure, that is, having an organizational history, is not to be underestimated.

FORMALIZATION AND INTERNAL RESOURCES

Some Necessary Distinctions

School personnel, probably like people in general, usually do not appreciate what it means for an organization to have a history. To passes a past is to have a social structure or "sets of alternative actions, or tendencies to act in certain ways... and the constraints that specify or limit these alternative actions", as one recent social scientist phrases it (Buckley, 1967). A major part of the origin of an organization centers on generating or building these sets of alternatives and the constraints that define them. We believe that this is the essence of Selznick's conception of formalization and we propose to explore it in additional detail, in the context of the origins of an innovative school organization.

Because our organization is an elementary school we have a special case. As compared with other organizations, a school has a rather interesting social structure. A major dichotomy exists in the age of its members, since the adults are concentrated into a subgroup of teachers and administrators. In addition to age, one also finds power, freedom, knowledge, and maturity concentrated among the adults. This adult faculty is also a minority. Also the school is a part of a larger organization, the school district. The school's purposes are a particular kind of socialization. Its technical base is open to high debate. Its environmental relations are political with local control. In such manners a school is a special kind of organization. Hypothetically, the processes of formalization will vary because of these differences. A well-developed comparative theory of organizations would have solved some of our problems here.

As often occurs in trying to formulate a difficult problem, the resolution, in retrospect, is absurdly simple. Organizational change is a broad rubric requiring its own set of concepts. It might be analyzed into purposive and nonpurposive antecedents. The beginning of a new organization is a special case of orvanizational change. Consequently, principles appropriate to organizational origins ought to be special instances of the more general principles of organizational change. Similarly, developing an old organization is a special case of purposive organizational change. Maintaining an innovative organization, by definition, involves dealing with planned change. Starting an innovative organization is a compounding of the two special cases of genesis and innovation.

Although no organizations are autonomous in the sense of being independent of their environments, organizations do vary in the degree to which they are subunits of larger organizations. Once again, Kensington was unique. As a public school, it is a unit of the larger Milford School District. But it had a special relationship to the district; it was a "protected subculture." Relatively, it moved freely of many organizational constraints of the larger organization. It set many of its own goals and almost all of its procedures. It was probably as autonomous as any public school ever is. These unique aspects had special implications for the origins issues.

For instance, if a natural history of an autonomous organization were described, we presume it would have small beginnings—few participants, limited resources, and trial-and-error procedures for reaching its goals. The required decisions would be relatively simply and, as they occurred, they would be cummulated, examined, and formalized into social structure. Over time, specialized roles would develop, routine activities would be instigated almost automatically to recurring stimuli, and the members of the organization would be able to tell an outsider or newcomer about "the way things are done here." In time, the latter might carry a righteous or normative quality as well. The organization would attain a coordination of an artistic sort, much like the smoothness one sees in a highly skilled psychomotor performance such as diving, gymnastics, or golf. Considerable time and energy resources are involved in making the innumerable decisions that accumulate into a social structure which then serves to guide and to direct the participants and leads to economy in goal attainment.

Thus, at another level, this complex adaptive process may be viewed as involving "a source of variety against which to draw, a number of selective mechanisms that sift and test this environmental variety against some criteria of viability, and process that tend to bind and prepetuate the selected variety for some length of time" (Buckley, 1967, p. 128). Although the genesis of formalization may be gradual or rapid, we hypothesize that a new but autonomous organization may be gradual or rapid, we hypothesize that a new but autonomous organization moves through such a process of decisions, trial and error, activities, gradual growth and formalization.

In the general case, a school that has been created whole, in respect to full size of members, staff and pupils, and without a history does not initially have a social structure; but it does have ties with a parent organization. It is not totally an autonomous organization. Without this social structure, the new organization generally appeals more frequently to procedures and available documents, such as the formal doctrine, from the larger parent organization. Because Kensington was a "protected subculture," the ties to the larger organization, the Milford School District, were deliberately less than usual. In these sense, Kensington was more like an autonomous organization. Because the school was deliberately mandated to be innovative, the impact of the district's structure was also reduced.

The history-less, near-autonomous, innovative organization faces immediately a continuous series of decisions of the "problems of the moment." Inevitably, because of the complexity of the human condition, these decisions are conflicting to some degree. At its worst, on the one hand, this can precipitate staff confusion, frustration and, in many instances, emotionality. A lack of experience in key activities can be critical. The task of making the decisions especially in a "democratic" style can be a tremendously time-consuming and fatiguing process and can drain resources from other aspects of the organization. Each of these in turn can generate meetings and conferences and more drain in time and energy, a vicious circle that can be severely debilitating.

In an educational organization, major consequences can occur in the resulting confusion and disturbances in teacher-pupil relations. No one knows for sure just what to do; directions are not clear; and control of pupils is jeopardized. This is coupled with limited time and energy for preparation as a result of other meetings. In sum, the most severe consequence, a kind of anxiety, is created. Meeting a group of youngsters when procedures in teacher-pupil relations are confused, and when one has inadequately prepared for the lessons, qualifies as such a consequence. In part, we are anticipating later portions of our descriptive narrative, the early weeks of school in September.

Resources Limits: A Major Unanticipated Consequence of Formalization Processes

Early in August, a major problem began to arise at Kensington. It involved the expense in time, energy, personnel, and materials related to beginning this new, relatively autonomous, and innovative organization. Essentially, we are saying that all organizational change carries heavy demands for resources. Our special case of change, the origins of an innovative organization, makes the heaviest demands. If these resources have not been budgeted or if they are unavailable for other reasons, the organization lies in peril. An early observation and interpretation stated in this way:

Another item that came up in my discussion with Eugene concerned the lack of administrative assistance that he has. For an elementary school in which the principal just "keeps the wheels turning" and things going as they are, be doesn't really need a lot of assistance. That's an hypothesis. But for an elementary school in which the principal is trying to change a number of things, then it seems to me that he needs someone to help coordinate, communicate, follow through, and carry out the numerous and almost endless little details and chores. Eugene doesn't have anybody to do this, and he is being pushed back into a terrible corner with his other work and with keeping the program moving. This is related to Larry's point about having in the background of any innovative attempt sufficient budgeted resources to pick up all the slack and all of the difficulties that are bound to arise from unanticipated consequences. Administratively, it seems to me that Kensington School is headed for that kind of problem also. An assistant principal could handle some of this, or it might also be handled with the team leaders playing a much more influential role in this set of tasks. Part of the problem locally may fall around the inability of Eugene to delegate responsibility (8/18).

In short, we hypothesize that the phenomenon of beginning an organization, and especially an innovative organization, requires more resources than usual, and second, that the unanticipated consequences of each purposive social action will require an added increment of resources. Finally, we argue, the Kensington planners did not anticipate to the required degree either of these demands. In this discussion we believe that we are saying much the same thing as Etzioni (1966) in his use of the concept "take-off."

"The concept of take-off, borrowed from aerodynamics, is applied to the first stage of epigenesis to distinguish the initiation point from where the continuation of the process becomes self-sustained".

As he extends the analogy, he speaks of the resources needed for self-maintenance.

"The image is one of a plane that first starts its engines and begins rolling, still supported by the runway, until it accumulates enough momentum to 'take-off,' to continue in motion 'on its own,' generating the forces that carry it to higher altitudes and greater speeds. The analogue is that through accumulation, while relying on external support, the necessary condition for autonomous action is produced".

Al Kensington, the resources available for creating organizational structures and processes were limited. This aspect of Kensington's newness remained all year.

In addition, Kensington had several unique dimensions that intensified the consequences. These aspects can be drawn from our earlier descriptions also. They include: (1) the nature of the immediate goals themselves, for example, individualized instruction; (2) the lack of teaching experience; (3) the newness in many organizational patterns such as team teaching about which the profession has limited intimate and generalizable knowledge; (4) the "upside-down" authority structure; (5) the intrastaff conflict and negative sentiment; and (6) the more extended activities, for example, the Curriculum Committee and the staff research program.

Furthermore, we would hypothesize that the successful operation of an organization that lacks a set of formal procedures is greatly dependent on the use of verbal skills. The style of the team meetings grew from that of the early T-group training sessions. Interpersonal communication was to utmost importance. The analysis of past events, the diagnosis of student and faculty problems, the reactions to community sentiments, the clarification of intermediate and long-range goals, the means of attaining objectives, the ways to preserve the uniqueness of the school, and a minimum concentration on the "nuts and bolts" of the organization characterized a typical meeting. The records of the decision-making process indicate some of the communication problems. Discussion seemed to vary among, at least, four levels. The first was the theoretical; the second, the "nuts and bolts"; the third, interpersonal relations; and the fourth, personal anxiety.

Some of the great time demands of a system of this nature have been pointed out. Other than the time spent in instruction and contact with the children during the day, there were numerous meetings, may of which were both long and frequent. There were team, subteam, and total staff meetings. All of them were in addition to the regular teacher-pupil responsibilities, and they were not during school hours. It was not unusual for a team meeting to last three-and-one-half hours to four hours. Parent meetings, the parent-school organization, and the Curriculum Committee sessions also were attended in some cases by all staff members and in the latter two instances by a part of the faculty.

There were innumerable antecedents for what appeared to be the extra-ordinary amount of time devoted to the school. Kensington was new with no traditions and norms of its own to look to, to find security in, or to modify. Even more dramatic was the fact that the staff was to develop plans and patterns to follow with little or no help from other less innovative systems. Seldom were Kensington's reference groups functioning elementary school organizations. More usually, university-based scholars or selected "schools of thought" that represented what was to be attempted at Kensington filled the role. In a sense, ideas were their referents rather than schools already in operation. This is doubtless true of anything that is really innovative. However, many aspects of Kensington had been developed and utilized before the attempt to integrate them into an innovative whole in the Milford District.

Thus, with its absence of previously developed norms, procedures, and the attempt to modify what had been viewed earlier by other practitioners as solutions to procedural and instructional problems, perhaps it is not surprising that "building" the many intangible and agreed-on ways of doing things required so much time.

The notes provide various pieces of information as to the reaction of the families of the staff and, in turn, the faculty member's statements about their families. A half-dozen of them would include: (1) one member allegedly bought to color TV because of his many nights away; (2) another's wife commented about seldom seeing him and he jokingly responded that he was going to have to get a divorce if he weren't home more; and (3) other married staff's objections to a lot of evening and weekend meetings because of ill spouses and outside responsibilities in the district and in the larger community. A number of the faculty were unmarried; they rended to be strong advocates of the school's philosophy, and they were able to spend evenings and extra time on academic matters. Initially, they were also very interested in the Curriculum Committee, which met frequently and for several hours at a time. However, as the year progressed even they were less willing to devote large blocks of time to long team and committee meetings. The Saturday staff meetings also contributed to the time pressures. There also seemed to be an unspoken faith in contact and duration of contact with the building, with the ideas it represented, and with fellow faculty members. Yet, the believers in this same faith came to realize the millstonelike quality of the exhaustion and frustration that may come without respite from a responsibility and mandate so great as, "Go build a school", and the organizational corollary, "develop a formal structure" in which this will occur. We summarize these conceptions in Figure 2.4. As the figure shows, a number of events drained Kensington's resources. The processes leading to the selecting and testing of alternatives from the environment and emphasizing congruency with the mandate from the district level were critical. These expenditures were increased by the requisites accompanying implementation of innovative processes and goals. Also, as noted elsewhere, the low level of experience and formal teacher training combined with the lack of acquaintance among the staff and the lack of information about mutual capabilities, interests, and productivity to make further drains on scarce resources.

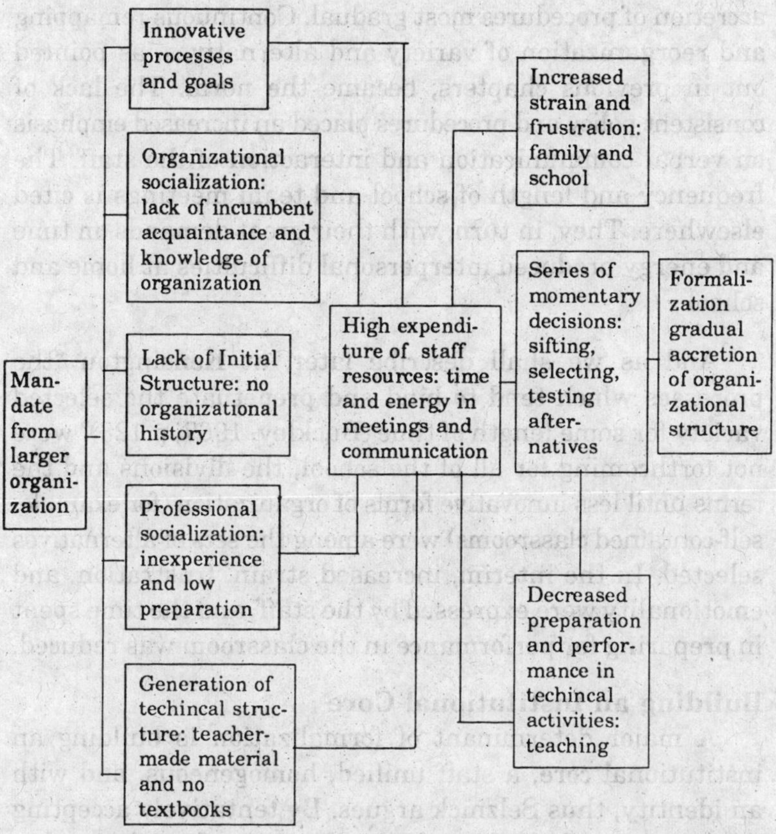

Figure 2.4. A miniature theory of resources and formalization at Kensington.

Often the alternatives that were selected were subject to conflicting interpretations, an outcome of high ambiguity about teacher-pupil role behaviors and increased strain and frustration for the stuff. Less time was available for preparation of materials for teaching which, in turn, was reflected in the performance in the classroom.

Although formalization at most provides a range within which certain activities may be performed, the continuous sifting and testing of elements from the environment made accretion of procedures most gradual. Continuous remapping and reorganization of variety and alternatives, as pointed out in previous chapters, became the norm. The lack of consistent policy and procedures placed an increased emphasis on verbal communication and interaction of the staff. The frequency and length of school and team meetings is cited elsewhere. They, in turn, with their great demands on time and energy produced interpersonal difficulties at home and school.

And as we shall describe later, at Kensington "the processes which tend to bind and prepetuate the selected variety for some length of time (Buckley, 1967, p.128)" were not forthcoming for all of the school, the divisions and the terms until less innovative forms of organization (for example, self-contained classrooms) were among the sets of alternatives selected. In the interim, increased strain, frustration, and emotionality were expressed by the staff, and the time spent in preparing for performance in the classroom was reduced.

Building an Institutional Core

A major determinant of formalization is building an institutional core, a staff unified, homogeneous, and with an identity, thus Selznick argues. By tentatively accepting this, we can ask for hypotheses clarifying the relationship of building an institutional core to the phenomenon of formalization for the data of our special case, the origination of an innovative organization. Our efforts will focus on two broad domains: (I) an analysis of the T-grouping experience, a very important innovative procedure for organizational socialization; and (II) "true belief", a way of focusing on faculty sentiment in an innovative organisation.

I. T-GROUPING: INNOVATIVE ORGANIZATIONAL SOCIALIZATION

Of all the analyses and interpretations, one of the ones we hesitated about most involved the T-group. As we have indicated elsewhere, our intent has been to create hypotheses that fit our case—our accumulated field notes. The hypotheses are offered then for wider testing and verification. The following analysis is an attempt to conceptualize T-group experience with an aggregate of staff new to each other, yet on their way to becoming a working unit.

Our problem of putting additional meaning in the interpretation of the training experience begins in the phrasing of the issue. Instead of asking the simple question, T-groups—pro or con?, we would ask, "What happens to an organization when the participants come together for the first time, engage in T-group activities for a week, and then must work intimately together for the next ten months?" To the best of our knowledge (Miles, 1959; Bradford et al., 1964; Glidewell, 1966) research has not been directed to this kind of problem. However, training groups are being formed with members of the same organization (Katz and Kahn, 1966). Miles (1964), in his discussion of temporary systems, presents a taxonomy that includes temporary staff and client, and permanent staff and temporary client, but does not present intensively the quasi-temporary system in which the client is permanent but the staff is temporary, actually the more usual consultant case. Nor does he handle the special case of the time at which the meeting occurs in the history of the organization. The intent of our discussion is to describe and to interpret this special case special case of T-group experience.

Initial Aspects

During the first week of the month's workshop a number of events took place that were intervened with the T-group experience. Some occurred in the meetings per se, and some occurred formally and informally along the way. We have tried to analyze and categorize them around several broad rubrics consistent with our general conception of organizations.

Negation of formal status . The T-group experience was new to the members of the Kensington faculty. In the judgment of the observers, the experience was dramatic and influential. For instance, although informality was built into Kensington in a variety of ways, the T-group experience contributed to this. As we have indicated, at the first meeting the faculty was grouped vertically, that is across divisions, into two groups, and the principal was a member of one group. It was at this point that he shifted his role to that of a peer, a member of his group. During a meeting containing a discussion of status barriers and problems accompanying them, he gave them the option of calling him whatever they felt most comfortable using—by title or by first name. One of the members quickly suggested that they call him by his first name; this was accepted by members of both groups, and throughout the year the principal was addressed by his first name.

This move toward informality had its limits, however. The principal's formal position was a factor that was impossible to overcome totally. This is true, we believe, because of the complexity of the special authority encompassed in the role, which we analyze in detail later, and partly because of the perceptions teachers have of principals. The summary notes that report on the conversations between the observers reflect this:

> I have had little chance to talk with Eugene about the progress of the workshop or, for that matter, about anything else in the program. Paul tells me that the principal's presence in the other group raised considerable difficulty with the

group's progress. When they split into small subgroups and he was not in one group, that group made tremendous progress in discussion and in moving toward a series of analyses (8/12).

Delineation of the faithful and the skeptical: public testimonials. Early Tuesday morning, the observer recorded several items of interest:

> Follow-up comments on yesterday seem necessary. One of these centers on the selection of people for the school. While I haven't had a chance to check it out carefully in the field notes, it seems to me that almost everyone has made a testimonial of some kind of extreme faith in the new school and what it is trying to do. The contrast here with the group of teachers at the Washington School is also very, very marked. The cruciality of this variable should not be neglected and should be highlighted in the general write-up of the report. It, coupled with the principal's enthusiasm and with his own very unique conception of the nature of elementary school organization and instruction, is an important variable (8/11).

Our interpretation that the T-group experience provided an opportunity for making public deeply-held feelings and beliefs. As we indicate elsewhere, the staff selection in an innovative school, the sentiment of enthusiasm, and the principal's Institutional Plan were salient early. Opportunities for expressions of faith, in one sense, helped to make somewhat less nebulous or organizational structure that was to become Kensington; however, the public testimonial statements also fostered an over-aggrandizement of Kensington. In reality many of the intangible doctrinal aspects—the verbal assessments and descriptions, both written and unwritten—of the facade were reinforced in this manner. The further importance of such public statements and acts of group members has been clarified by

Festinger *et al.* (1956) in their account entitled *When Prophecy Fails*.

Personal revelation. As we have indicated, the T-group experience was dramatic and influential. One aspect included what we have called personal revelation, the offering of intimate details of one's personal life. We described episodes of catharsis-type comments, psychiatric-type interpretations, and emotional rebuttals and defensiveness. There were discussions of the personal details of one's self system. Also there were discussions of several kinds of personal salary negotiations. For instance, the extra pay for the workshop and the breaking of the fixed salary scale, years of experience, and amount of training, in order to attract some of the staff, were items of comment.

Toward the close of the workshop, several weeks after the T-group experience, the observer recorded this interpretation.

> In one sense, the first week has opened up all of these other issues about who I am, where I am going, etc., which then can be used perjudicially toward one another. For instance, Bill Kirkham's obvious ambition might have been held under better check and better control if he had not revealed his "true goals" because of this softening up process. The question I have really is: Could he have worked with this group as a functioning member even though he held these other ambitions more latently? On the surface my guess would be that he could. It seems to me that this would be possible for Jack Davis also. And, in one sense, it seems to be that he's defined his role that way. He will not be involved as an assistant academic counsellor although the majority of the others will be. Another idea that this has cued off concerns the report that several of the people had been developing strategies for resisting Bill and dealing

with him in many of the things of the things that he was proposing (8/31).

The aftereffects of self-revelation, for example, vulnerability, frustration, and anxiety (especially among the ISD team members), were to be felt all year long. In that respect, the T-groups legitimated individual catharsis. The input of this information had consequences for the individual making the statements, the individual attending to the statements, and the organization that now contained the information as part of its accumulating history.

Emotionality: sentiments as group tasks. Many items could be used to illustrate the principle that the T-group provokes high emotionality among its members. One part of this occurred as the T-group trainer interpreted a group member's behavior and pushed him toward insight and resolution. In the summary notes, the observer recorded the episode in this fashion:

Perhaps the most dramatic incident occurred late in the afternoon when the leader began interpreting some of the behavior of the members of the group. She accused one member of not learning from his experience of yesterday and taking over the group again at noon, as he had, and of making decisions for the group. This led to good bit of defensiveness on his part and soon opened up another who commented how angry he had been at this. He related how he hadn't said anything and he wasn't going to say anything all afternoon and how he had responded only on the direct request of the first. He was mad at himself for doing this also. The leader "egged them on," with more interpretation and also urging, to have the second ask the first how he felt rather than just assume that the first would be unhappy if the second had made a comment. This took three or four urgings. A number of people chimed in during this.

Later, one member ultimately called them all "chicken" for not wanting to fill out the questionnaires regarding the T-group functioning. The leader made a very dramatic interpretation of a third's behavior, which was rejected almost completely. At the close of the meeting, the first commented to the second that he hoped they could sit down and talk for a while today because they were going to have to work together all year this year. Most everyone seemed to be provoked at each other or at the whole training program by the time the day was over. Paul commented about much of the general hostility that existed in the other group and how most of it seemed to be directed toward the leader rather than toward each other. As far as I can tell, very little hostility is directed toward the other leader at this time (8/12).

In one respect, being socialized in this fashion made the task of divesting suggestions and ideas from the idiosyncratic characteristics of their originators even more difficult. Making affect manifest, in a group working together through time, does not necessarily insure in later task sessions that it will "make way" for the presentation of substantive concerns. High emotionality, generally acknowledged to be minimized by formalization of organizational procedures, was highlighted and, in part, legitimized by the early training groups at Kensington.

The degree of acquaintance. As one might suspect from our discussions of testimonials, high sentiment, and personal revelation, the T-groups produced also an intimacy, a high degree of acquaintance among the staff. The observer reflected on the contrast in this and a group workshop of which he had been a part.

Another phenomenon that really hit me was the discussion that several of the staff had during one of the small group sessions. The depth and the ease with which they could talk with one another at this point is truly very remarkable. The function of the T-group in having people share a variety of more personal and intimate aspects of their lives as they bear on the school creates, or at least seems to create in this particular instance, a kind of Bill Mauldin *Up Front* degree of rapport, for they have been at war and have fought together. They were pretty sick of having so much small group-connected things, and Sue particularly commented that she wants to go off for a month without any connection with the group. Bill Kirkham is talking about the possible kinds of sedition that he can engage in, which strikes me as very unusual for him, although in might not be. This might be contrasted with another group I participated in, which, in some respects, never did get far enough along after six weeks to discuss issues very well together (8/13).

Thus, in an instance where a staff is unacquainted, a training group experience seems to be a method whereby participants may learn certain aspects of one another in a relatively short time. However, overinvolvement in the intimate, personal facets of group members' lives can be a hazard. Later, as is pointed out elsewhere, these intense personal dimensions often seemed to reappear as obstacles in working together.

The T-Group's Longer Reach

The T-group experience, as we have described it, was a potent experience during its week of operation. In our judgment, its potency reached far beyond the first few days. In this section we trace out the further implications of the experience. As we have described in our methodological section, the ultimate test of our interpretation must lie in the accumulation of similar cases and ultimately in experimental analysis. Nonetheless, we can relate data from our notebooks, our interpretations at the time, and, now, later reflections.

Content-less-ness of the T-group? We argue that the T-group has a special kind of content instead of being content-less. At Kensington what it seemed to do was to cause some people to "play out their hands" in an unfamiliar game or in an unfamiliar way. In general, this then set up a social structure that was not transferable to the central tasks of the elementary school, even an innovative one such as Kensington. Our initial speculations are mixed with earlier problems and several lines of inquiry:

> This is another aspect of the T-group experience that intrigued me very much. Insofar as there is not an agenda, the major resources, to use their term, upon which one can draw is an individual's own identity, stabiligy and general empathy. There may be some other factors such as one's more self-oriented needs. The kind of thing I think I'm saying is that you may get a selection of some kind of an index of maturity coming out of this kind of group which typically you don't get as quickly or as dramatically, if at all, from other groups. Once again; Tom seems to be the guy who is coming out on top in this. My guess is that Kirkham is not able to do this and that he is much more visible as somebody trying to feather his own nest and push his own status. That may be more my own personal bias than the group's bias, although I doubt it. His "take charge" kind of attitude, which may have been very effective in rural Ohio, somehow just is falling flat here. His deflation is apt to provoke some very serious problems.
>
> My interest is seeing the development of a faculty social system is coming to pass in very fashion. It makes me wonder how much of this kind of thing occurred at some distant point in the past at the Washington School downtown. My guess is that once the group had achieved some kind of initial stability, the sort of thing that I witnessed regarding Mr. Alton is about as close as this would ever come. Then the individual must struggle with the group rather than

struggle with the aggregate as the aggregate tries to become a group.

I would have some real questions as to whether this is the best kind of experience to start off with, or whether it would be better to work a week and then have this and then work a couple of more weeks. Paul and I raised a point somewhat similar to this when we talked about having some subject matter much less sensitive than the individuals, own egos and the developing group structure as the immediate task at hand. This just loads the dice for a high effective involvement and possibly the setting up of hostilities and sensitivities that will be forever in getting dissipated. It's an interesting question as to whether there are any data whatsoever on the T-group experience as it applies to a new group that is not an *ad hoc* group but that will have long-term continuing relationships with one another. Also this was a new experience for the training staff. Lois, the first Sunday night, said that she had never worked with a group exactly like this in just this kind of situation. Lynn had not either (8/12).

We have spoken about the high emotionality of the T-group experience. The serious problems associated with Kirkham's removal were described earlier. The consternation over task focus versus process focus remained throughout the year. The social structure that developed during the group sessions was in most respects not applicable to the tasks specified in the mandate of "building a school." This social structure often contrasted with the highly formalized doctrine.

The process-substance dichotomy. When approaching a new task like that of starting a school, people vary in their preferences. Some want to explore verbally the totality and some want to begin on a particular concrete problem and let this take them to the more general issues as well as to other concrete problems. In retrospect, this variation in style of approach to large significant novel problems seems to be a most important dimension of human personality. One facet, although not the central aspect, was caught partially in the observer's notes in the Sunday night planning session:

> Another item that occurred which left me a little bit uncomfortable was the lack of concern about the immediate desires of the people for a lot of information about the new school and about what they would be doing and how they would be doing it. Eugene has put this off until the second or third week rather than having it in the first week. This is a very interesting commentary on the staff as the staff perceives him for the moment. It will be interesting to see how much of this keeps cropping up in the discussions as we go alone. Lois' notion here was that informational questions could be treated and answered as they arose. She had not bought the cult so directly that she felt it was impossible to do this. Lynn was even more open about it and talked about the value of having an informed member who could act as a resource on certain questions of fact. (8/10).

Ultimately what was created was a schism between those faculty members who wanted to talk about the school in general—its objectives, its ideology, and its broader contribution—and those who wanted to talk about specific roles, specific duties, and day-to-day items of "What am I am going to do?" A variety of dimensions seem to run through this: the realist versus the idealist, the practical versus the dreamer, substance versus process, and deductive versus inductive.

A major hypothesis we would offer states that neither the global nor the concrete leads to "better" solutions. In effect, we would argue that each ultimately digresses into the other, in the give and take of group interaction. Essentially there are assumptions of compromise, taking turns in expressing opinion and points of view, and freedom to participate. Our date suggested that the T-groups accented one line of approach. In effect it provided a normative pattern by reinforcing the processual and abstractly oriented individuals, and delaying and frustrating the concrete and substantively oriented individuals. This tended to develop subgroups in the faculty, to make the easy give the take between individuals more difficult, and to set the occasion for serious conflict which was to erupt later. The notes suggest this:

> At noon I had a brief conversation with Bill about his experience in the T-group. He has never done this before, and the way he talked left it clear that he wasn't very happy with it. Paul told me that his conversations with Jack, Bill, and Dan indicated that they also were getting concerned about having a whole week of this when in their eyes there was so much work to be done. I did talk briefly with Dan at lunch, and he commented about the concern for group process without regard for content. He argued that the kind of content, or what I would call the task, would probably make a good bit of difference in the way in which the activity was carried out. He wondered about how generalizable the experience would be in that regard. As far as I know, he hasn't taught except for practice teaching.

One of the more interesting things that happened in the discussion this morning concerns David's holding to the notion of getting the objectives laid out before you can talk about the specifics. On the one hand, it seems to me that this is one sensible way to make decisions and lies behind some of the comments that we are making in our analysis of decision-making. It also strikes me that he has a strong intolerance for the fact that some people have to operate in a different style. Specifically, it conflicts with Jack Davis' interest in going from a set of concrete examples to a more general framework. If you like, one could make a case that this inductive approach is actually more in accord with the Kensington set of goals than actually starting out rationally with a broad set of goals. Later Jack raised the possibility of people retaining convictions and yielding to action which makes the compromise move along. This issue was one that got considerable discussion earlier and one on which they couldn't reach any fundamental agreement. This fits in with the earlier comment, since David seems unable to accept other people's methods of approach and to make compromises and to work with them. My guess is that he would interpret this as a lack of authenticity and also as a lack of being his real self. This kind of inability could lead to real havoc with the Independence Study Division (8/12).

The T-group experience in conjunction with the problem-solving styles formalized the dichotomization of the staff and introduced serious frustration to the "inductives." This is turn led to intense staff conflict and helped precipitate what was to be a permanent schism in the ISD and the ousting of Bill Kirkham, which we have called the Kirkham incident.

Avoidance of the mechanics. One of the consequences of the T-group experience, the doctrine, the enthusiasm, and the biases of several of the influential persons on the staff was an avoidance of the procedural means, the "nuts and bolts" issues, as the staff came to call them.

A number of items came up late this morning and over lunch. For instance, at the lunch hour I raised the direct question, at seemingly an appropriate time, as to whether there would be report cards at the Kensington School. None of the group—Tom, Bill, David, Liz, Alec, or Jack—knew whether there would be report cards. They are all, or nearly all, operating on the assumption that the cumulative records with anecdotal comments and work samples would be used to show the parents the kinds of things that the children are doing. No one has any notion as to who would carry out the parental conferring.

As they responded, no one in the group seemingly has thought much about it or tested it out very extensively. There also is a lack of clarity on articulating with other schools regarding transfers in and transfers out (8/19).

Later that same day the observer commented:

Another point that keeps coming up and reflects my own bias about organization and administration is the need for mechanism to attain certain kinds of goals or ends. This was perhaps best illustrated in a discussion this morning with Sue and Liz and Alec about the phenomenon of their overlapping interest in the integration of knowledge being presented to the students. The several people involved in the conversation were all agreed that content integration was important. There was some agreement that part of the content integration would be a consequence of a basic attitude that would prevail throughout the school. However, there was little discussion and seemingly little awareness of what I would call the mechanisms to help make this happen. Specifically, I mean the kind of planning that would go on, the kind of distribution of the time of the teachers and the students, the pinpointing of responsibility for initiating and following through on agreements, and so forth. This may be part of the negative transfer from last week. but as far as I can tell, there is practically no concern on the part of the younger people about this phenomenon. There seems to be some pleasant assumption that once we all get to know each other, then it will automatically happen. This is precisely what I don't agree with. Perhaps this view-point reflects my more general concern for the mundane. There are some exceptions to this in the Independent Study Division. I think the major people who would take exception are Jack and Irma and perhaps Alec. The Basic Skills Division might also be exempt from this. The Transition people have not really spoken enough for me to know. Perhaps the more significant notion is that there is a time and place for both. The staff who are resisting feel that we haven't gotten to that time or that place as yet (18/19).

As our early descriptive accounts indicate, the workshop time did not progress rapidly and easily with these concerns. Critical procedural decisions were being made late in the August workshop. Therefore, it may be hypothesized that in innovative attempt in which procedural details are initially unspecified, further avoidance of mechanics (that is, lack of attention to planning, scheduling, grouping, subject matter concerns, distribution of materials, and spatial arrangements) becomes a key variable for the consideration of organizational consequences. As was indicated previously, the training groups fostered processual concerns and, in part, ingitimized the avoidance of planning for specific and concrete organizational activities and tasks.

Individual captivation. Although the T-groups captivated several of the staff, David found it most congenial. It permitted him to engage in broad philosophical discussions, in explorations in the quest of self-understanding, and in entry into close personal relationships with fellow staff members. The approach to learning, which the unstructured position provided, fit his point of view in working with children. Generally, this consisted of informal relationships between teacher and student, a minimum of didactic or usual instructional behavior with large groups off children, and a high regard for the internal motivation for learning. It blended neatly with his perception of the Kensington doctrine of individualized instruction and gave a substance to the vaguely defined role of academic counselor. As our descriptive account indicated, it led, also, during the first week to a new element in the ISD (Independent Study Division) program, T-grouping or group processes with the children. The intent here was to aid the children in exploring their interpersonal relationships which, in turn, would enable them to function more fully as individuals and as members of ISD teams. The pupil T-groups produced a number of unintended organizational consequences.

Summary. In our judgment the T-group experience was a very powerful technique. The timing within the year, the close relationship to parts of the formal doctrine, and the salience for individual staff members were part of the context. The implications were both immediate and long term. A number of our most signifying hypotheses regarding this innovation at Kensington are summarized in Figure 2.5.

It is possible to view the events of Kensington at a considerably more abstract and general theoretical level. For example, if innovative attempts, such as our case of Kensington School, are characterized by what March and Simon (1958) call unprogrammed activity, then uncertainty as a variable is more potent and the presence of uncontrolled outcomes is greater than in traditional programs. Less is known about the variation in inputs; that is, when a large number of innovative elements are introduced, priorities in terms of degrees of influence are more difficult to assess. As is noted elsewhere, high uncertainty also may be accompanied by a degree of vulnerability, an openness to output threats, not present in settings in which participants may be better able to specify both inputs and outcomes. In one sense, the training groups, as Figure 2.5 shows, were implemented to reduce uncertainty about both group functioning and individual performance with the group. Search behavior such as this has been treated by some analysts as a quest for identity, a search for knowledge or information that identifies at the levels of the individual, the group, and the organization (Klapp, 1969). Also, the training groups were selected as a part of the formal socialization of members to enable them to become a part of the quest for a "new" elementary education. Although the quest may be treated at this point as an organizational goal, our later discussion dealing with true belief also explores its ramifications for the individual participant.

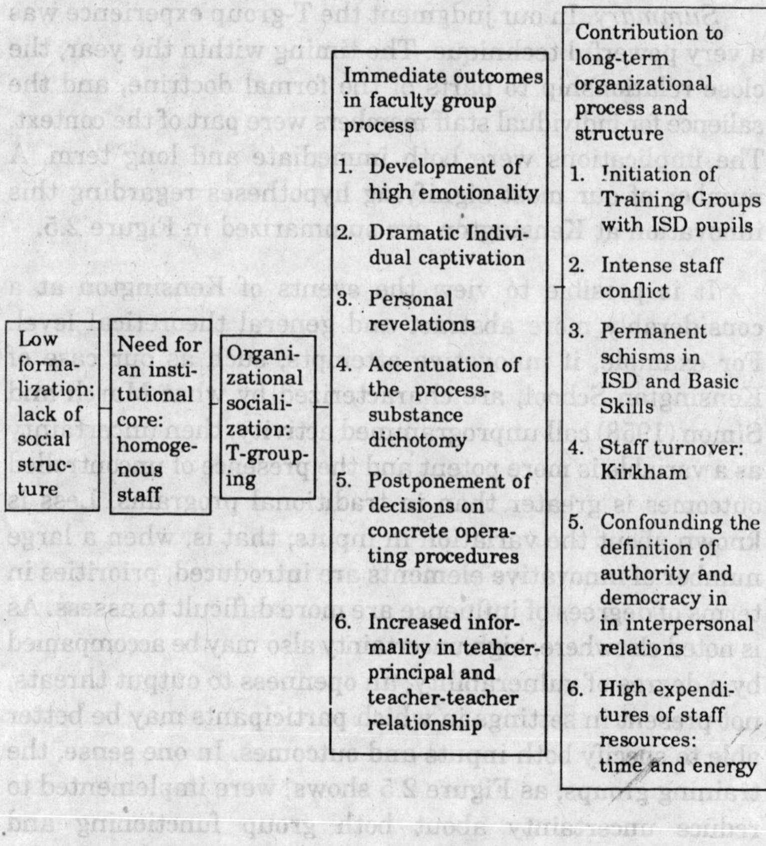

Figure 2.5. The context of T-grouping at Kensington

In short, these events of early August and the accompanying analysis suggest some of the nuances in the building of an institutional core in an educational organization which has an innovative thrust. With such a focus, one perceives clearly a number of problems that organizational theorists and administrative practitioners would do well to anticipate.

II. TRUE BELIEF: STAFF SENTIMENT IN AN INNOVATIVE ORGANIZATION

Introductory Perspective

The use of the T-group as a means of building an institutional core, a homogeneity of outlook and sentiments, was a in important part of Kensington's strategy and program. But people come to organizations with existing sentiments. If our data from Kensington can be generalized, we would suggest that the sentiments brought to a highly innovative organization are a special, different, and idiosyncratic kind and, as such, are an important aspect of the anatomy of such an organization. As we were a part of the Kensington experience and as we tried to analyze it, the emotional quality loomed large. From the first day of the summer workshop the observers noted the quality of excitement, enthusiasm, and high aspiration. This section of the analysis becomes a consideration of sentiment, a broad rubric that has been defined by Homans (1950).

"Now let us go back to our passage again and consider another set of words and phrases: sentiments of affection, effective content of sympathy, respect, pride antagonism, affective history, scorn, sentimental nostalgia. . . . Here we shall call them all *sentiments*, largely because that word has been used in a less specialized sense than some of the others, and we shall speak of *sentiment* as an element of social behavior."

Our particular concern is with sentiment within the dynamics of a beginning, innovative organization that is also a part of a larger organization, the Milford School District, and a larger system of ideas that we have called the "new elementary education."

In a seminal book, *The True Believer,* Eric Hoffer states the proposition: "Some kind of widespread enthusiasm or excitement is apparently needed for the realization of vast and rapid change..." Elsewhere he describes the extreme of enthusiasm and excitement is embodied in an individual: "...the true believer—the man of fanatical faith who is ready to sacrifice his life for a holy cause . . . . The parallels between our observations of sentiments in an innovative school and Hoffer's more general argument suggested an important opportunity for mutual stimulation. Our developing analysis could test the conception offered by Hoffer, and his ideas could serve as guides for additional insights. As always, the field notes arbitrate the differences.

Finally, in attempting to understand how the sentiment of true belief functioned in a beginning organization, Klapp's (1969) consideration of the sources and attributes of crusades and crusaders helps. Some of his interpretations correspond to what we observed, but others suggest additional hypotheses that need verification. A crusade may refer to "any remedial enterprise undertaken with zeal and enthusiasm." Both in terms of its program being a remedial one and the great enthusiasm that accompanied implementation of the ideas, the events surrounding Kensington resembled those of a crusade.

3

Innovative Organizational Socialization

Although Kensington had been developing for several years, it began, in a real sense, for the staff in August. The teachers' first formal contact as a group occurred then. The four weeks between August 10 and September 8, the official opening of the schools, constituted a workshop and served as a period of initial socialization. As will be described in some detail, the activities were varied and the implications of those days August were crucial for the development of the school as a social system. A month-blong workshop was a major educational innovation in itself and an important part of the overall Milford innovation strategy.

The first five days were spent in Training Groups led by representatives from the National Training Laboratory (NTL). Two sessions per day involved the total staff and the remainder of the time consisted of group meetings. The training groups were viewed by the leader as a form of planning for the coming year. The staff was to "begin to be a group" they were to get to know one another, to learn each other's resources and to learn to work together.

Monday, the first day of the second week, began what the principal called the "big day," the end of the preliminaries of general planning (by all kinds of other persons and committees), and the beginning of intimate work by the staff. The week contained also a more intensive welcome, which we characterized earlier as the mandate, by the Milford superintendent, Dr. Steven Spanman; total staff discussions led by the principal; the arrival of a consultant, Dr.Roberts, from City University; and the beginnings of a working committee structure. The latter included horizontal committees, devided according to age levels of the children—Basic Skills Division (first and second grades), Transition Division (third grade), and Independent Study division (fourth through sixth grades)— and vertical curriculum committees, in science, language arts, social studies, and mathematics. A more general committee, the Curriculum Coordinating Committee (CCC) was established. Finally, considerable time was allocated to individual work by the teacher. Each teacher kept an activity log that was turned in to the principal and that provided information for him .

Much the same pattern was followed during the third week.

Although the same activities were continued during the fourth week, the focus shifted toward preparation for the temporary physical quarters and planning by the teams who would be working together. The new school building had not been finished on schedule; consequently, Basic Skills would be housed in six rooms at Milford High School, Transition would be in Hillside, a neighboring elementary school, and ISD would be in the gym of the Milford Junior High School. Also the broader environment impinged on Kensington. The total district staff came alive as they prepared for their teaching responsibilities in the September beginning of another school year. The Kensington staff spent two evenings meeting with parents in a discussion of the school and its program.

On Tuesday, after Labor Day, school began.

The Faculty

Although we do not have data on faculty composition of new schools and, consequently, cannot make rigorous comparisons, our belief is that the Kensington staff was unusual and unique. First, the majority of the teachers were new to the school district. They were recruited from the breadth of the Midwest—the Gulf of Mexico to Lake Michigan. This meant that they were not only new to each other but also to the procedures and practices of Milford. In the eyes of the administration this meant they could be trained directly in the new procedures instead of having to break old habits and patterns prior to retraining.

Following though on the same concern with breaking old ways, the staff was relatively inexperienced. Seven of the original twenty-one had had no teaching experience beyond student teaching, an apprenticeship, or internship. Although two of the teachers had had more than 20 years of experience, most of the remainder of the staff had taught less than five years; even some of the ones who were older had come to teaching late, after raising their families. Interestingly also, three of the group had had almost no training or experience with elementary children; they had trained for secondary education in one of the content areas. The group in ISD, especially the resource people, had been selected because of intensive training in speciality: science, mathematics, social studies, language arts, and physical education.

The staff seemed very able intellectually. Three of the group had all their doctoral course work finished and needed only a dissertation. All of these three had taught at the college level; one additional staff member held a part-time, Saturday morning college position, a Principals and Methodes of Teaching of course. Most of the staff had M.A.'s (some through an ,M.A.T. internship program). The quality of the intellectual life and discussions among the staff in committee and faculty meetings we found impressive relative to our contacts with other elementary schools.

Attitudinally, the faculty was characterized by the one of the central office staff as "not a Republican in the group." Although our conversations and informal interaction suggested this was not true for several, the majority reflected a liberal Democratic political orientation. More specifically, however, the group did have high scores on the *Minnesota Teacher Attitude Inventory*(MTAL) (Cook *et al.* 1951); the median fell at the 85 percentile on the national norms for elementary teachers. On the *Teacher Conceptions of the Educative Process* (Wehling, 1964; Wehling and Charter, 1969), the faculty scored high on pupil autonomy, teacher consideration, adjustment as a goal, content integration, and closeness of teacher-pupil relationships. Although the validity of these measures of teacher schemas, beliefs, and attitudes might be questioned, they have achieved widespread usage. According to the intentions of the test authors, such scores indicate that the Kensington staff was chosen in harmony with the formal doctrine. The high MTAI scores reflect teachers who are:

". . . able to maintain a state of harmonious relations with his pupils characterized by mutual affection and sympathetic understanding. The pupils should lide the teacher and enjoy school work. The teacher should like the children and enjoy teaching. Situations requiring disciplinary action should rarely occur. The teacher and pupils should work together in a social atmosphere of cooperative endeavor, of intense interest in the work of the day, and with a feeling of security growing from a permissive atmosphere of freedom to think, act and speak one's mind with mutual respect for the feelings, rights and abilities of others' (Cook et al., 1951, p. 3).

The Wehling-Charters scales indicate that the Kensington teachers valued pupil autonomy as both an end and as means. They saw pupil personal-social adjustment as an important goal. The academic content should be relevant and integrated. Teachers should be psychologically close to the pupils and considerate of their wishes, needs and interests. The summary field notes from the first few days of the workshop capture further emotional and attitudinal characteristics of the faculty.

There is a very real aura of 'We can do it and what we're doing is very important. It's very much in the creative front line of educational practice and innovation". This is all very striking for the teachers were trained in a variety of places. Several of them came from City Teachers college and spoke glowingly of their program their which was in contrast to many of the others who came from 'better universities' and the comments they had about their education programs. There are some real questions as to why these people haven't been stifled the way some of the preservice education students were in other situations. Most certainly there is an ability factor here, for these people seem more than a little bit bright, and some of them seem very, very able. It is also critical to get a notion of Eugene's background, since yesterday he commented that he had spent last summer as supervisor in the Harvard-Lexington program. Apparently he had kicked around in and about this kind of a program for some time.

Another thing that I'm struck with, and it may be just because I don't know our own students as well, is the degree to which these people, and particularly the young ones, are excited by the kind of thing that they are doing in education. Our students at City University just do not carry this flavor of excitement. I am sturck, too, by how much of this, and the references to which they appeal, especially people of the order of John Goodlad, are known and are not widely discussed, at least among the staff at City University. For instance, my colleagues, if they mention goodlad, usually mention him in a condemning fashion. We have, in effect, abandoned this kind of approach or set of variables and, at lest in my case, without having considered the evidence, which my colleagues would probably say did not exist, and without careful argument about the programs. I guess the point I want to make is that there is an excitement about teaching and about the things they are going to be trying, even though they are not very specific and clear about this yet, that pervades the place and that I just have not seen in any degree at City University. Such an influence or consequence alone would seem to me to be so meritorious as to argue for its inclusion almost regardless of the validity of the position. That one will need to be straightened out in some detail (8/11).

Of the original group, nine were men. All but one of them were married. Of the twelve women, seven were not married. In only one instance were both husband and wife members of the Kensington faculty. Such a high percentage of men on an elementary staff also seems unusual.

The staff contined five non-certificated personnel, four married women, and a young man just graduated from high school. He served as audiovisual technician; the women served in the capacities of secretary, library clerk, teacher aide, and instructional clerk. They were all new to their positions. At the time, this extensive use of aides and paraprofessionals was also quite novel. Later, during the fall semester, four student teachers from local colleges were a part of the staff. They were finishing the final year of their teacher training program. Again, although we do not have comparative statistics, this seems to be a large number relative to the total staff size.

Although other personnel, from the central office, custodian staff, and cafeteria personnel, were part of the story, they tended not to be central actors. As the staff changed during the years and new persons played a vital part, we have introduced them in the following chapters.

In short, the administrators of Milford had assembled and unusual group to staff the Knsington School. They were young and inexperienced, but bright, enthusiastic, and attitudinally focused on the central tenets of the new elementary education. An initial congruence with the formal doctrine had been achieved.

The T-Group Workshop

Training Groups, described by the NTL trainer as "the exciting venture of the learning to become a group" began the first day of the workshop. The focus on Training Groups arose primarily through the efforts of the principal, Mr. Shelby. The T-group activity involves a unique kind of learning experiencc in which a number of persons meet together and the activity of the group develops out of the growing relationship among the members of the group. The training is intended to make individuals more perceptive of group processes and their own personal relationships within the group. general sessions alternating with the T-group were to combine lectures, discussions, and training exercises using human relations problems.

Considerable discussion among Shelby, the principal; cohen, the district curriculum director; and the two NTL trainers arose in the decision regarding the constitution of the two T-groups. The alternatives considered were a split by division (ISD versus TD and BSD) or a vertical split; the latter form was selected. The principal was to be in one group and one of the older, more experienced staff members, tom Mack, the curriculum materials coordinator, would be in the other. The men and women were divided about equally.

An additional degree of the novelty of this experience became apparent in the discussion Sunday evening before the workshop began.

Another point that came out at this time was that neither Lyn nor Lois, the trainers, had had an experience with just this kind of situation before, that is, in the sense that they were working with groups of people who are now an aggregate and have not worked together and who ultimately will become a long-standing and continuing group. Each of them has worked more with *ad hoc* groups and secondarily with groups that had a history and would remain together. But the no-history phenomenon seems a very unique one (8/10, 7:00 a.m.)

In effect, a group of people who had not known each other before and who were to work together all year in a formal organization, a public school, would be spending their first week together in a T-group setting.

The schedule of the Training groups was much the same for each day of the first five days of the workshop. In the morning hours, the two groups met independently; after lunch, there was total group lecture an discussion. The lecture content on Monday centered on people's varying perceptions and expectations; the genesis of these differences, for example, past experience; and the consequences of the differences, for example conflicting values and loyalties. The discussion was lively and controversial. After a brief coffee break, the T-groups met for the remainder of Monday afternoon, until approximately 5:00 p.m.

The content of the day's T-group discussions involved getting acquainted, raising questions about specific aspects of Kensington, and the giving of interpretive comments by the NTL trainers on aspects of group process. In one group, the initial focus lay on the problems of status an authority in both teacher-teacher relationships and teacher-principal relationships. For example, a possible dichotomy of younger versus older teachers was raised. Being free to challenge the principal and to call him by his first name were examples of the latter. In the other groups, in the middle of a discussion of leadership, one teacher interrupted with, "Idon't care who is leader. I'm interested in 'nuts and bolts', what will go on in Kensington." The situation was entangled in two additional ways. Earlier, another teacher had commented that the training groups lacked reality in that they did not have a task. Later, one teacher argued that they should develop their own expectations. He was supported by comments such as "We, the staff, are the architects." Incontrast, another felt that they should await direction from the superintendent and principal.

The T-group was not a situation responded to with indifference and docility. A brief summary comment recorded late Wednesday after the third day is typical:

The morning T-group session and the afternoon T-group session each had its dramatic high point. In the morning it involved a fracas between David, Joe and Lyn. David was opening himself up catharsis fashion. Joe made an interpretive comment that cut right through to the nature of David's personality. This material was on tape and Lyn cut in about this point, indicating that it was much more clinical and therapeutic than processual, and it had gone beyond the limits of what we felt qualified to handle. Feedback this afternoon from Paul indicates that Tom thought that she should not have turned off the tape recorder. His feeling was that it was personal but not disabling and that she could not handle that material intellectually instead of emotionally. Paul also reports the other group perceives our group as having all of the aggressive leadership and the fireworks. They feel that there isn't any leadership in their group. Paul sees this as centering on the inhibiting role of Eugene. Paul reports also a noon conversation in which Jack was very angry in talking with Dan about the salary revelations that have occurred and that fact that he was under misinformation. Most of the locals were under misinterpretation also about the $300 that they would make this summer (8/12).

The more extended theoretical analysis of these events will be developed in a later chapter.

During the remainder of the week of Training Groups, attention centered on analytic observations of group behavior, discussions of group-related variables (individual effectiveness in groups and its determinates), problem solving, communication, decision-making, and leadership. Authority and the contrast between the authority structure of Kensington and that in other elementary schools was considered.

Not unrelated to authority and decision-making, the concept of the "Institutional Plan" was introduced by the principal, Shelby, during the week of the Training Groups. The Institutional Plan was presented as a given, and it was indicated that a serious problem would arise if personal goals were radically different from the plan. He indicated that effort had been made to select staff that would in effect erase the line of difference. The givens were commitments by the school district to persons or institutions both outside the school and outside the district, such as the United States Office of Education. Also, in response to those interested in "nuts and bolts" and task concerns, the principal lead an extended question-answer session on the new building (which would not be ready for opening day), materials, supplies, procedures, and the like. Questions of audiovisual use, music schedules, and modern math in the curriculum were answered as undetermined as yet; their solution was a goal of the summer workshop.

At the end of the week, when the T-group reconvened for the last time, the intensity of the emotionality was indicated further as the groups talked through the pro's and con's of continuing to meet during the course of the year. For several of the group, the experience had been a dramatic revelation of self and an intense development of empathy. Others viewed it as a social situation leading to further important social situations at Kensington. At 2:20 p.m., the total group met for the discussion of issues in forming a new group, establishing working relationships, and ambiguous and unknown aspects of the teaching role. to facilitate the transition into the following weeks, the three divisions—Basic Skills, Transition, and ISD— met independently. The groups engaged in tentative exploration of themselves, the T-groups experience, Kensington's program, and the temporary facilities. Prior to adjournment, the groups met together for summary discussions.

George Homans (1950) argues that the interaction demanded of people by the formal organization spills over, becomes elaborated, as sentiments of mutual liking are perceived. This elaboration takes the form of new activities, increased inter action, and more broadly based sentiments. This was the case at Kensington.The field notes on Wednesday contain an entry that indicates some of the early sentiments:

Part of this morning's T-group conversion centred about the salary problem and its effects on teacher relationships. Jack was rather surprised to learn that others knew his contractual agreement with Milford School District. In the course of the discussion with Eugene, some of the women made known that they were not aware of the fact that they being paid to attend this workship. Jack expressed some concern in the morning workshop that the rest of the staff was fully aware of his exact salary picture. During coffee this discussion was carried on at greater length. He sated in very clear terms that it made him very aggravated to know this. Dan was also present and both he and Jack agreed that it was their opinion that this is an entirely personal matter and no concern of anyone's as to their salary (8/12).

Later in the same day's notes, the cross currents subgroup interaction and evaluation were reported.

During lunch I participated in a conversation with Liz, Elaine and Dan. By consensus of opinion these three felt that it would have been advisable to begin the group action by working on an actual problem instead of by studying group processes. Elaine stated that she would have preferred working on an actual problem such as the curriculum and then coming back to studying group processes at a later time to analyze what they had done(8/12).

Still later in the notes of the same day a 'minor' event was reported:

At the conclusion of today' T-group, Jack left the room, thereby somewhat disrupting the conversation of the group. It was undecided whether to continue. However, the conversation did continue and was centered on this main point: Should they analyze the day's discussion or should they wait until the entire group reconvenes tomorrow morning? The group gradually began discussing activities of the afternoon session and Lois, the trainer, interrupted to remind them that they had suggested to wait until tomorrow morning's session. By group consensus they decided that this was the wiser plan: consequently, they adjourned (8/2):

The salary issue concerned not only the Kensington staff but other teachers in the district who thought it "unfair" that Kensington teachers were paid above the stated training and experience guidelines. The concern over the T-group and alternative ways of beginning the workshop was to crystallize later into a conflict between the "substantive' versus the "process" staff orientations. The final point, when do we stop talking about school "business," who must be included in these discussions, and who determines when faculty come and go, were issues about which no precedent existed, and which were to be a part of the issue of influence and decision-making in the school.

Although our major analysis of the implications of the T-group experience appears in the next chapter, we can report that one immediate reaction of the teachers was that of considerable discomfort. The first item of the first Staff Bulletin on Tuesday, August 11, stated the response this way:

"We are very pleased with the progress of the staff orientation workshop. *Although a group development laboratory is never a comfortable thing to participate in* (our italic) it should prove helpful to us as we work together during the year to provide a forward-looking educational program. As important as the many tasks for preparing for opening of school are, we believe that the development of good working relationship among the staff is of primary importance" (Bulletin No. 8/11).

The last item of second Bulletin, issued on Friday of the first week, summarized the reaction.

"We would like to extend a special work of appreciation of the directors of our group development laboratory, Dr. Lois Erickson and Miss Lyn Karson. *We will not deny the frustration of the experience, but undoubtedly it will prove have been most profitable as we work toward our goals this year* (our italic . . . . Thanks again for your contributions in providing experiences which will certainly be long remembered".

The Middle Two Weeks

The big day. The second Monday, August 17, was described as the "big day" the beginning of intensive substantive discussion and planning for the year. The principal chaired the total staff meeting. Initial discussion centered on several major items, one of which was the interdependence of the program parts. The principal developed a lengthy analogy that contrasted the functions, methods and parts of a T-bird an a Model-T ford as he spoke of Kensington and traditional education. Commitment by the staff was stressed. This was analyzed as issues of staff selection and the congruency between individual philosophy and instructional objectives. Also, a contrast was made between tradition authority and a "rational approach,' which was to be used at Kensington. These were construed as conditions developing commitment. The principal accented the latter. The introductory remarks of the principal stressed skill in implementing the program, the necessity for making mistakes, and the possibility of staff growth. "The Institutional Plan," the principal's document, was raised "as a skeleton of the program, and the staff is to put hair on it." Finally, he suggested that differences and disagreements should be open and explicit. They should be "out on the table," as had been accented in the previous week.

The remainder of the pre-coffee discussion centred on two mimeographed sheets containing job descriptions of the academic counselor and the subject specialist and a third sheet that illustrated the administrative organization of Kensington. They are reproduced these documents provoked a brief discussion that focused on (1) an administrative organization different form the single , self-contained class as a means to handle individual differences of pupils; (2) who makes what decisions regarding the academic program; (3) criteria of progress from division to division; (4) Goodlad's (1963) models of instruction, A,B and C; (5) Kensington as an attempt to be a "C" school; (6) the nature and kinds of educational objectives for Kensington with the emphasis in the effective (self-motivation) and complex intellectual skills areas; and (7) decisions yet to be made regarding particular books, materials and supplies.

Further aspects of the schedule were clarified. For the remainder of the workshop the faculty was to meet as they deemed necessary—by divisions and in curriculum committees. They were free to schedule themselves and their meetings, and they were to note the times on a bulletin board. Subsequent to this, faculty members asked to indicate which of the following committees they would like to be on; (1) materials and facilities, (2) curriculum coordination, or (3) curriculum subcommittees in (a) language arts, (b) mathematics, (c) social studies,(d) science, (e) creative arts, and (f) physical education.

A final item concerned 'practicing what we preach." The staff was to be on individual schedules with the principal as their"academic counsellor."

They were asked to fill out daily logs on their activities. Discussion ensued as to who would read the logs, and at the suggestion of a staff member they decided, in order to facilitate communication, to have them open to everyone.

As is pointed out elsewhere, the logs completed by the faculty were identical in form to those required of students a few weeks later. Thus, in the second week of the workshop, primary attention was given to substantive concerns. At midweek Dr. Leslie Roberts from City University met with the faculty and began an extended consulting arrangement.

The institutional plan: a phrasing of the formal doctrine. Earlier we had a good bit to say about the formal doctrine, the codified ideology of Kensington. The antecedents of the doctrine, the dimensions of the doctrine, and the consequences were part of that analysis. During the weeks of the workshop, the Institutional Plan, Shelby's statements of the Doctrine, became the focus of considerable discussion as well as the major operational plan for the development of the school. Briefly, the central thrust of the school was to assist pupils in becoming "fully functioning mature human beings." This goal was to be reached through "individualized instruction." The latter was not to be merely differentiation in rate of presentation of materials, but differentiation in content as well, that is, according to the needs of the individual child. The curriculum was described as "spiral," and it was to accent processes instead of content. The materials were to be individualized rather than packaged as textbooks. Teacher-pupil relations were to be reformulated form categories such as "restriction of pupil" to "freedom for pupils," form "teacher responsibility for teaching" to "pupil responsibility for learning" and from a "closed, rigid social climate" to an "open flexible social climate." The organization was to move from six rigidly defined levels or grades to three divisions. Within the divisions, teachers were to play differentiated roles. In turn, the pupils were to change from being "passive" and "reactive" to being "active" and "initiating."

The divisions. The divisions, or as they came to be called by the staff: Basic Skills, Transition, and ISD, were an important and early definded division of labor. These groups began working together in the second week of the August workshop. Instead of describing in detail the development of the divisions, we present an introductory overview from the observer's notes of his perception of the way things stood as of mid-workshop, 4:00 p.m. Tuesday, August 25.

I had a chance to spend a fair amount of time with the Transition Division. By all odds, they are the most smoothly functioning team in the school at this point. Each in his own quiet, unpretentious way makes suggestions to which the others listen as they go about shaping up a program. Apparently they are interested and pleased in what they have been doing for they do not want to bring another person into their group now. They explicitly told this to Eugene, the principal. Shifting them to their temporary quarters in Hillside School came about with no great difficulty in terms of Eugene's suggestion, or in terms of their acceding to it. My guess is that they will be a very task-oriented set of teachers who will have all kinds of interesting things for the kids and who will blend their own suggestions and initiations with the suggestion and initiations of activities from the pupils. They seem to make judgments on a reasonable common-sense professional background basis. The only major inhibiting factor that I see at this point is that Claire and Dan have not taught extensively. Meg may be a bulwark here if she is as good as I would guess she is.

The Basic Skills group seem to be laboring with the consultant, Leslie Roberts, who is pushing them hard, and who seems not to understand that they are now a team of four and a team of two rather than a six-man tea, Carla seems very set in her ways and is going to do what she wants to do, and apparently Mary will integrate without too much difficulty. The other team looks like it might go also. My guess is that Elaine is, an old warhorse who is a very experienced, a very agile, and a very interesting teacher. Jean has had enough experience to know her way around, and Wanda seems also to be a very stable person. It seems that they will be able to carry Sue well enough until she learns the ropes. If she turns out to have some talent for working with young children, the group then should be able to move along without too much difficulty.

As I summarize the teams, it becomes very interesting that the major reservation seems to lie within the Independent Study Division. Paul reports that David was in a quiet and unhappy looking mood all day to day today. He also reports, as I think I indicated earlier, that Liz has made all kinds of comments of her unhappiness with David and with the way in which the group is going. Perhaps this is the item that upset David. I have no data on that. As I recall now, one of the gals called David on a couple of things yesterday. They had to do with his railroading the group. This may be also a reason for his quietness. In this group also, Irma is very unhappy, and she is apparently thinking of dropping out of team. She feels she is less adequate for it now than she was when she discussed it last spring with Eugene. She has been unable to get any kind of a structured role so that she will know what she's going to be doing. Although nothing arose today that I saw or heard about, Kay has a continuing problem of wanting to support David and at the same time seeming to side intellectually with some of the people in the disciplines. This makes here seem to vacillate back and forth between varying points of view. Jack seems to be frustrated in terms of wanting to act like a principal and run the meeting. He and Alec look like people who have interests in teaching rather than in some of the other kinds of activity that teachers might be called on to do. Alec has had minimal experience.

The staff left a bit earlier than usual this afternoon. May be it is my own feeling, but it seemed to me that everyone looked pretty tired. Unfortunately, the group has had so little experience generally and almost none in extended team teaching that they are now at the point of waiting and seeing how things begin to develop. They don't realize the kinds of preparation, a la Joe Grannis' chapter in the Shaplin and Olds (1964) book, in which they might be engaged that would be helpful for the long term haul this semester and year.

Also, they still have many procedural problems on how to work together. This seems, in part, to be a function of Eugene's inability to relize that the school is part of a bureaucracy and must have some of these overtones and, second, that the week of "sensitivity training" is having all kinds of negative transfer effects (8/25).

The committees. Although the first week was characterized by the Staff as the T-group week, the later weeks of the workshop were dominated by the committees and the divisions. Cumulatively these events had their immediate consequences and also their longer effects. The number of committees and committee assignments was quite large and contained overlapping memberships:

1. Curriculum Coordinating Committee (7 members)
2. Curriculum Subcommittees
   - (a.) Language Arts (4)
   - (b.) Mathematics (4)
   - (c.) Science (4)
   - (d.) Social Studies (5)
   - (e.) Creative Arts (5)
3. Facilities committee (4)
4. Research Committee (5)

Some of the complications of the committee structure appeared in the summary notes early in the third week.

One of Paul's first comments was of the order, "What goes on in the central committee?" His observations, independent of anything I told him, were that the role of the central committee seemed to have changed dramatically, and that it has taken on a number of different functions that it did not have before. He was curious as to how these changes had come about. Specifically, the kinds of things that he mentioned centred on what he called the committee serving as a sort of an assistant principal to Eugene. In effect, they have considerable power and they are being used as an instrument for a variety of policies. I asked him directly about Engene's behavior, and he commented that Eugene, in effect, was leading the meeting and was running it. I asked him "like an administrator?" and he commented, "yes." This, in effect, corroborates the behavior I saw earlier in the morning in the same committee. Paul indicated several specifics: listing the agenda items, instrumenting them, and terminating discussion on items when he thought there had been sufficient discussion. To my direct question, Did he sit around and wait for an agenda to develop as has occurred in other meetings, Paul responded "no" (8/25).

The summary notes record not only thefts in leadership styles and role within the faculty, but also the complications of dissatisfaction, disagreement and ineffectiveness. We began a paragraph with a prediction.

Both of us keep expecting the lid to blow off the whole place when the anxiety of the first day finally mounts with the realization that they aren't organized. This is our prediction, however. Related to it now is a conversation with one of the teachers who is extremely irritated at several things: (1) what she perceived to be railroading of items, (2) the inability of anybody to get anything done in the committees, and (3) the tremendous amount of committees that she is on—at least, three. A close to verbatim quote went something like, "If things don't straighten out very soon, I'll pack up my bag and go home." This was followed by "you can quote me too" (8/25).

Without presenting our detailed documentation, suffice it to say that the committees did not produce authoritative position papers. The dilemma of a totally individualized child-selected curriculum as opposed to a structured and sequenced set of experiences formulated by adults was not resolved by the curriculum subcommittees. The curriculum coordinating committee had a turbulent history, changed its name to the central committee, and became, during the workshop, the arena for most of the open struggle for power and leadership in the school.

The kirkham affair. On Friday, August 25, at the end of the third week, Kensington underwent its most significant trauma: Bill Kirkham was removed as a member of the staff.

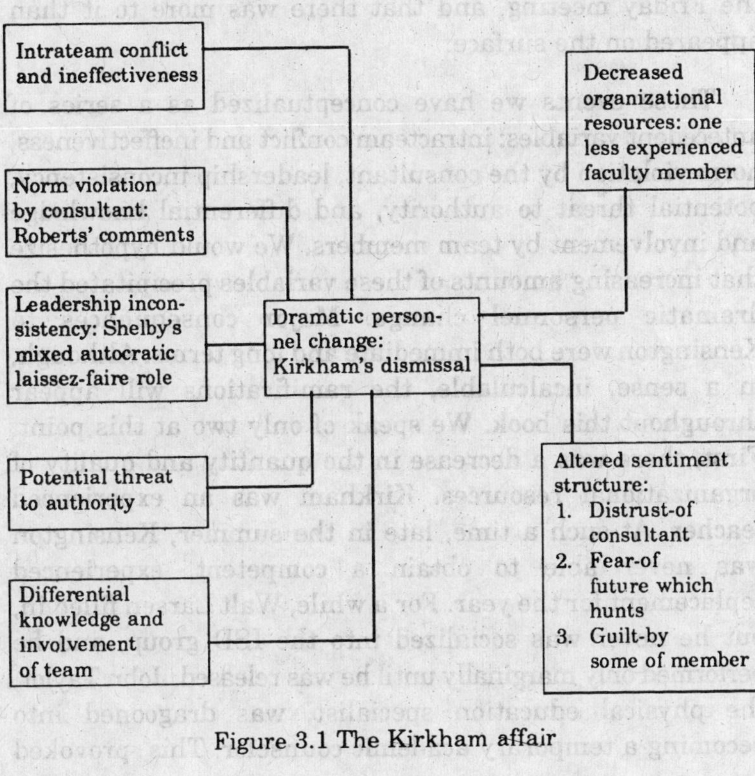

Figure 3.1 The Kirkham affair

The action occurred, formally, during the ISD team meeting. The stated reasons were that his point of view was too different and that he blocked the smooth functioning of the team. Varying opinions existed about the genesis of the action. Some of the staff were more cognizant and involved than the others. Some thought the action had been handled well; others did not think so. There was some feeling that the unsettled team leader role was critical. Some thought that Leslie Roberts behaved inappropriately in his consultant role. Others believed the dismissal arose as a scapegoating mechanism because of the failure of the team to progress. Some thought the Bill and his curriculum ideas were a personal threat to Eugene. There was talk that Bill did not know it was coming, that he thought it was arranged before the Friday meeting, and that there was more to it than appeared on the surface.

These events we have conceptualized as a series of antecedent variables: intracteam conflict and ineffectiveness, norm violation by the consultant, leadership inconsistency, potential threat to authority, and differential knowledge and involvement by team members. We would hypothesize that increasing amounts of these variables precipitated the dramatic personnel change. Major consequences to Kensington were both immediate and long terms. Although, in a sense, incalculable, the ramifications will appear throughout this book. We speak of only two at this point. First, there was a decrease in the quantity and quality of organizational resources. Kirkham was an experienced teacher. At such a time, late in the summer, Kensington was never able to obtain a competent, experienced replacement for the year. For a while, Walt Larsen filled in, but he never was socialized into the ISD group, and he performed only marginally until he was released. John Taylor, the physical education specialist, was dragooned into becoming a temporary academic counselor. This provoked some ill feeling in the other divisions (to which he had a responsibility) and reduced resources in that phase of the program's concern for the totality of the child's personal development. Second, within the ISD team, major shifts occurred in the group-sentiment structure. Specifically, an increase in distrust, especially toward the consultant, developed. An atmosphere of fear occurred as rumors of future witch-hunts seeped or exploded through parts of the team. Finally, guilt was now a part of the group, as some members of the team had second thoughts about the event. Figure 3.3 diagrams these hypotheses.

The Final Week of the Workshop

Time falls naturally into weekly units that have ascertainable beginnings and endings. Events often correspond to this naturalness, although August's lingering one more day into the new week seemed to carry overtones of the prior three weeks. Although the Milford District was mobilizing itself through a district-wide teachers' meeting, which the Kensington staff attended, and Kensington was to have its first evening parent meeting, the spirit of William Kirkham remained.

After the district-wide morning exercises of speeches, introductions of new staff, and announcements relevant to the whole district, the Kensington teachers as well as the other teacher returned to their individual schools. On Monday afternoon, Shelby met with the ISD teachers and they spent a half-hour discussing aspects and implications of Kirkham's removal. They then moved to the task of delineating a new organizational pattern. The academic counselor and subject matter resource specialist roles reached "clarity" around points such as: (a) the academic counselor will concern himself with the totality of the child's development; the subject matter specialist primarily will concern himself with development in that resource area; and (b) the academic counselor will decide whether the child, for instance, goes to science, but will not decide what will be done in science. Shelby commented that the biggest responsibility of the academic counselor in the first month would be helping the pupils learn to work independently and interdependently. Decisions were reached to have the children form groups of six as the basic unit. Irma and David were to be the academic counselors. John yielded to pressure to become a "temporary" academic counselor, and this was changed later to an assistant academic counselor. Liz and Kay became assistant academic counselors and resource persons in language arts and social studies, respectively. Jack and Alec remained resource persons. In the eyes of one of the staff, ISD was working better with Shelby's active leadership.

On Monday evening, two parent meetings were held in Milford. One, a large protest meeting, reflected continuing community and sistrict conflict with the public schools. The specific issue involved a book and fee assessment that had been levied against each pupil. The roots of the community conflict had a long history: a prior superintendent who had been fired and rehired, a split in the school board, and a reputation in the regional area as "a district with problems."

The second meeting, which was repeated on Tuesday and Wednesday evenings, was a Kensington parents' night in which the principal and staff sought to explain the program. In a pleasant style the principal spoke of the need for understanding between the parents and staff, the organizational structure of the building whose goal was to facilitate individualized learning, and the materials, books, the equipment that they would have available in the school. The parents expressed concern and confusion regarding bus schedules and knowing where and how the very young children promotion, grading and report cards. There were distinct variations in over all hostility of parents; Monday night was quite strong, although the other meeting went more smoothly. We discuss this in more detail in a later section on the organization and its environment.

As teams and as individuals, the staff continued preparations during the middle days of the week. The Basic Skills Divisions was meeting explicitly as a team of two and team of four. The BSD-4 team had drawn and cut out a "magic bus" which was to be a focus of initial activities. They were having a difficult time handling it because of a lack of bulletin board surface in their temporary quarters. Perhaps underestimating their accomplishments, they spoke of the day as "not very stimulating or productive." The Transition team worked on their plans for the coming week while the tile men resurfaced the floor in their large room (which had been a storage area for Hillside and the Milford School District) and the glaziers replaced glass broken from vandalism and informal play in the adjacent area behind the school. The ISD team alternated between working separately on specific tasks and meeting as a group. It was on Wednesday morning in the team meeting that the pupil Training Groups ideas, initiated by Shelby and responded to warmly by David, was instituted after a brief discussion of discipline and the need for pupils to move from external discipline to internal controls and the self-initiation of activities.

The Wednesday discussion, as recorded in the field notes, went this way:

David. We must internalize the goals of Kensington in the child and I think this can best be done by group process.

Kay. I agree very much, but will just discussion in small groups do this? This would be abstract.

David. I think discipline is not abstract. It is a very real issue. Children will come to a variety of conclusions and I would question how they came to this decision.

Eugene. I feel a teacher will be needed with the group like Lyn and Lois (the August trainers) were with us. Perhaps you could take a small group.

David. I don't care. I do think it is most important though.

(David questions the group as to their response).

Alec. I can see it at first, but I feel it requires close supervision—I think, it's part of the goals of the school, but I don't think they can do without us at first.

Eugene. How about letting David do this in small groups for the first few weeks and you all take the rest of this.

Shelby suggested that the faculty have one of the trainers, who was in their August training-group session, come to and assist them with the pupil training group. Kay and Alec expressed positive sentiments toward the idea of bringing in a trained person; however, David, who hoped to be most instrumental in setting up and continuing the groups, voiced less approval than did the others.

4

Innovative Teacher - Pupil Relationship

As the mandate, institutional Plan, and the discussions in the summer workshop have indicated, the relationship between teacher and pupil were to be innovative. Although "non-traditional" describes these relationships to some extent, a number of quite abstract terms were used. Non-graded, individualized, democratic, pupil centered, flexible, shared, open, purposive, free, and supportive indicate their tenor. Instead of attempting to clarify these terms, we remain at the "data level" in presenting a descriptive narrative of two critical points in this strand of the Kensington experience. The opening days of school in the temporary quarters and the move to the new building in December were important times.

The Initial Confrontation with the Pupil

The opening of school, the initial confrontation with the pupils on Tuesday, September the 8, began the second major phase of Kensington. The months's workshop, a major innovation in itself, had come and gone and with it the T-grouping, the many committees, and the varied planning. The physical plant of the new school had not been finished. Predictions for the completion ranged from several weeks to a semester. The divisions were to go their geographically separate ways, since they were housed in three temporary settings: Milford High School, Milford Junior High School, and Hillside Elementary School. The distinctions between "normal" school beginnings, about which there is almost no careful literature with which to make comparisons, the processes unique to the Kensington formal doctrine and program, and the consequences of the temporary setting remain difficult to tease apart.

THE INDEPENDENT STUDY DIVISION

Day One

School began in the refurbished gymnasium at 9:10 a.m., as the first busload of children arrived. The final organisation of the room, dittoing of instruction sheets, and so forth had occurred during the weekend. The effort, energy, and direction of David Nichols were paramount in this preparation.

The temporary physical plan in which the Independent Study Division began operation left a good bit to be desired. The main area was a large open gymnasium, located in Milford's Junior High School. Highboy and lowboy cabinets were available for partial divides, and other moveable facilities were accessible. In the room without permanent walls were 200 students, roughly from age nine to eleven. With them, according to the formal statement, we two academic counselors, four academic resource persons, one physical education resource person, a materials specialist, and an audiovisual technician. In addition to the gymnasium, the Independent Study Division also had use of a wide corridor with windows along each side. Faculty desks were placed in the hallway along with some tables for individual study and projects, and one area for instruction. A stairwell leading to the basement also was used for pupil Training Groups and small instructional groups. The playing floor of the gymnasium was covered with pieces of plywood that were taped together and that, with wear, would begin to pull apart. The student rest rooms were shared with junior high school pupils and were located in the main part of the building away from the gymnasium.

All of the teachers arrived early with the exception of Walt Larsen, Kirkham's replacement, who came at 9:15 a.m. The staff spread themselves out to usher the children from the buses, through the hallway, and into groups of six located somewhere in the large room at the children's own discretion. Most of these groups seemed to fall along sex lines, and along age and grade levels, as well as friendship. The following field notes capture in general the interaction of the first day in the Independent Study Division.

9:20 a.m., A quick of station area indicates that most of the group of 6's are along sex lines.Only one group in about ten is missed at this point Kids move down the line reasonably easily. Jack and Kay help. John and Walt get the athletic equipment sorted out.

The noise level continues to rise slowly as the number of children increases. The temperature and humidity also seem to be increasing gradually. Liz, for instance, is very warm and predicts some of the kids will be ill. 7 a.m. At least one parent is angry over buses: "I've been trying to find for two weeks," she comments.

Tom and Arthur are in the hall. Alec is at the door. Kay and Jack are at the tables. Irma is in her rooms. Mrs. Beacon is at her desk, registering, etc.

9:30 a.m., About one-half dozen tables are empty. Probably one more busload is due in. The teachers are milling about. Walt is still filling out a schedule. A mother is here with her son and with a baby in arms. She talks to Irma. Leaves her son. Tom drinks a cup of coffee. Kay asks me if I've got "chaos" written down yet.

9:40 a.m. I'm in back of David's area. Kay, Liz, David, Jack and Alec circulated from table to table helping the groups get started. Kay does this with consummate skill.

Tom is in to help also. The teachers are all very warm. The children gradually get the idea what to do and start making name tags.

9:43 a.m. John and Irma break their group into two parts. John has his in south hall. Irma stays in the gym. She has them pull out the blue sheet on miscellaneous information and begins to explain its contents.

Later in the morning, after a cup of coffee, the observer tried to grapple with the totality of the sense impressions coming in upon him.

10:45 a.m. I'm back from coffee. The sign-up for classes is going full blast, 8 to 10 groups. David is holding his first T-group. They're reading the *Weekly Reader* or a similar paper. A brief survey indicates the kids are milling all about the gym; the sign-up area is jammed. Half-a-dozen kids are in line at the water fountain; some exploratory behavior in and out among the high-and lowboy cabinets begins. Also there is some horseplay—poking, tripping, and hide and seek. Some children sit at tables and gaze about. The 11:00 a.m. T-groups start to assemble. David directs Arthur to tell them to wait in Area 3. Some of the kids, one group of girls, are playing volleyball on the playground. Jack, Kay, Alec, Arthur, etc., help kid sign up.

11:02 a.m. as I wander about and talk with individual groups, most seem to have some of the scheduling accomplished. A few sit and wait because the sign-up area is too crowded. Some of the younger kids seem especially lost. One group of older boys is frustrated because they have four things in but can't work in the fifth—which is P.E.

To this point, the only formal instructional activity I've seen is David's group reading the *Weekly Reader*. All the others are trying to solve scheduling problems. So far no tempers are frayed nor do I see any serious discipline problems. Teacher help by going from group to group and trying to keep kids moving along on the schedules. Major instructional activity will be this afternoon.

The noise—mostly the chatter of the kids—continues unabated. I personally am about to get a headache.

11:10 a.m. the gaining of attention of a total group, that is, the ones cared for by an academic counselor, is extremely difficult. Irma taps pencil on desk but this is pretty much in vain. Her group picks up chairs and moves to the resource area. She obtains cooperation easily, talks quietly to individuals, dyads and triads.

A final exert from the field notes continues our attempt to picture concretely the easy the first morning went.

11:35 a.m. I'm spending just a moment or two in David's T-group. No one says anything. He sits. The kids (4 boys and 3 girls) writhe around literally and look like chained, muted animals. They don't seem to know what's happening. They look like they want to leave the situation. Some keep looking down toward sign-up boards. Mostly they look restless, uncomfortable, bored and hot.

11:50 a.m. I continue to circulate. Several groups in the north area of the gym have obtained reading books and are making desultory overtures at reading. On girl comments—"This doesn't seem like school." Another child reads a copy of *Children's Digest* that she brought from home. Some of the boys draw draw airplanes and tank war scenes. There is a tremendous amount of listless behavior. Kids are sitting and not quite knowing what to do. At this moment only 2 of the 15 groups I see are reading.

12:05 p.m., on the south side three groups are reading. Four groups (3 of boys, and 1 of girls and boys) have come up with modeling clay. They are excited as they pound, roll, and form, the clay. Snakes, lady in a bathtub, and a pistol are some of the products. The kids push the forms into a glob and make something else. In general, there seems to be less of the listless type behavior here. John and Irma keep at it steadily. On the other side, David is with his T-group; Jack sits in the hall to prevent kids form going to the rest room during the junior high lunch hour. Alec and Liz have been at sign-up boards. Kay is tiring.

The TV is on over by the south wall.

Late in the afternoon, the observer returned form brief stops with Transition and Basic Skills. The notes indicated the close of the day in ISD.

3:30 p.m., back at the junior high and ISD.

Confusion still reigns. Kay has let her group because they would not do anything. Alec is teaching a math lesson. Essentially, he is asking "How many ways can you write the number 10?" He's got a long list of eight on the board: 4+4=8, 5+3=8, 3+5=8, etc. The assignment for tomorrow is the ten's. They can make posters or other art-type projects. He wants I am to bring these in next time, and he tells them of games and other activity that they can do in resource centre. He asks them to schedule him once or twice more this week. A minority of the kids seem rights with him. Many, however, seem vague and far away. Background noise is loud. Some kids are running, etc. He asks them to plan when they want to come in and what they want to talk about. He'll have a schedule ready tomorrow for the remainder of the week. He tosses out a variety of suggestions.

3:55 p.m., the group breaks up to go back to pupil stations, the desks where they store their materials.

3:55 p.m. in Irma's section, most of the children are filing out their work sheets. She and John move among the children and help them by answering questions and giving directions. As I wandered about, a group of boys were at each TV set. Size varied from about two to twelve. A few of the older and brighter kids seem able to handle freedom and work along on their log sheets. Others talk and wander.

4:05 p.m., the staff seems exhausted. David indicates there will be an 8;00 a.m., staff meeting tomorrow morning. The children are practically unsupervised. Irma is at a CTA (Community Teachers Association) meeting. Tom has a half-dozen pupils he's talking to. Liz is wandering still. Jack has been out in the hall. Arthur and Mrs. Beacon distribute bus tickets and an envelope regarding health (I think). Alec also has kept away from stations. The noise continues full blast. A few kids sign up for things.

The teachers have reported that the kids forget times they have singed up for. A few comment that they do not want any more language arts, etc.

There has been some scattered painting with watercolors, and a few of the pictures have been posted about. Some of the kids have watched a lot of TV, some have stood in the cool south starway. There has been very little P.E., this afternoon. No one has been on the field since I've been back. I checked, and Walt has scratched off the last hour and one half.

4:13 p.m., kids start toward the doors. The buses are not here as yet. Almost all of the kids have *a* book and their packet of papers.

4:20 p.m., the kids are lined up in the north hall for the buses. No one knows when or where the buses will come. Alec handles the major disciplining of quieting them and calling out bus sections. David, Tom, and aides help line up the kids.

4:45 p.m., buses arrive.

The observer noted early in the morning of the first day that the children were all "well dressed and well scrubbed". Later he commented on their social behavior:

It's now 5:00 p.m., the buses were one-half hour late and did not arrive until 4:45. The kids stood around in the hall and some in the gym for the half hour as they waited for the buses. Essentially they were a very orderly bunch who did not raise much difficulty at all. I'm continuously struck at how different the children are from the last year at the Washington School (see Smith and Geoffrey, 1968). The nonsence and the horseplay of a year ago just doesn't appear at this school. The defiance, the surliness, and the hostility are not present. Here, the teacher can leave the children unsupervised and they don't break out in fighting, name calling, and antagonisms. The "instinct of aggression" has been either bred out or trained to of these children. This contrast is one of the most instructive things thus far about the experience here at Kensington (9/8).

Continuous Reorganisation

The Independent Study Division did not reach a simple equilibrium. Continuous reorganization of both staff and pupils was the mode of approach as long as they remained in the temporary quarters. Each change, as we shall argue later, brought a series of unanticipated consequences with which the division then had to cope. We enumerate the sequence of changes and include brief excerpts of notes to define this aspect of ISD.

The original organizational structure. In the discussion of the preschool workshop, the framework of ISD was spelled out. Basically, the Institutional Plan and supplementary documents (Figures 3.1, 3.2,) specified that there would be three academic counselors and four resource persons. Each counselor was to engage in diagnosing, grouping, scheduling, and evaluating approximately 70 pupils. The resource or subject matter specialists were to provide individual and group instruction, develop instructional activities and materials, and engage in curriculum organization. With the removal of Kirkham at the end of the third week of the summer workshop, and with the brief but significant delay in replacing him, ISD reorganized into its opening framework.

The second structure. The crucial elements of the second structure, the first reorganization, we have described partially in the events of the first day. The pupils were organized into groups of six. The groups scheduled their activities on sign-up sheets posted in the central area of the gym. Some of the pupils spent a part of the day in Training Groups. At the close of the second day of school, September 9, plans were made to change this structure.

The possibility that students might not yet be able to work in a program that emphasized considerable pupil responsibility had not been fully taken into account. When the staff spoke of changing pupil roles, they seldom considered equipping the students with techniques that would insure facility in performing the new roles. In effect, the immediate student performance was overestimated. This was most clearly illustrated to the staff by the difficulties in writing the students logs and the difficulties with group scheduling. The logs were a daily record kept by the each student. They included what classes he attended, something about what he had done, and his feelings about the work. Each student was to have one-half hour at the end of the day of complete his log. With regard to the first day and the logs, one teacher observed that she "had a good many who couldn't write and they talked about how they couldn't fill them in." Another mentioned that some of the younger students were unable to fill in logs by themselves and "hardly with supervision." Still another noted that there was" no trouble when they're with one of us. The other time is hardest."

A further part of initial pupil difficulties involved the scheduling of classes. Subsequent problems were viewed by some of the faculty as having their origins in procedures the students were to follow. How the pupils were to "sign up" for instruction was not uniformly perceived by the faculty. Originally the students were to be grouped by friendship instead of by interest; however, some were not in groups and, thus, were unable to schedule with a group. They were described as "running around a lot and not having schedule forms." Group membership as seen as a problem: "Some are not functioning with the group at all." The scheduling was, phrased in to doctrine, a "strategy for making sure pupils assume responsibility." However, as pupil confusion related to scheduling within groups came to be viewed as problematic, were differences among the faculty as to whether programming should be focused on the group or the individual. Even within the groups, as was noted, there were difficulties involving the laxness of pupil acceptance of responsibility. John expressed a general sentiment based on the observation of the students the first two days of school: "Most haven't experienced this (scheduling). Some had a ball watching TV. I know a girl who spent two hours viewing it." Jack and Alec agreed about the children who had been watching television. The transcription below shows the way of most of the ISD Team were handling similar situations in the early days of school:

David. (in response to John). What did you do?

John. I asked about their groups. I tried to question them about the best use of time.

David. That's my feeling and approach. I ask to meet that group for 15 minutes and try to work it out in structure of the group.

John. Up to a point this works . . . Lots needs to be done if it will function at all. The group is the basic unit if it's significant.

David. I tried to make it clear. It is important that they learn. Group pressure is strong.

Alec. One boy was in a T-group half the morning; three others were in the other half. The group can't function at all.

Eugene. The small group is not the best basic unit.

Alec. I told them not to come as a group, but to schedule as individuals accordings to interests.

Even when students were permitted to "sign up" individually regardless of the action of their group, some were still unable to perform the procedure. Prior to the decision to have a self- contained classroom for those who had not mastered scheduling and the preparation of logs, Eugene stated that, "you get freedom when you assume responsibility. Should we have controls and put some in a situation until they do?" Jack asked: "Could we develop a list of pupils for a self-contained setting? Would that solve the problem for those who can't assume responsibility?" The discussion continued:

David. I have no objection, but do not place them indiscriminately. Some are struggling like hell.

Eugene. Where's the burden of proof? Will we put them in before they've had a chance to prove themselves?

Tom. This is the way we work with children at home.

Irma. When do we start? first we had no brakes and then we put them on. We started with no controls. It's lots harder now. It's easier to loosen up rather than tighten up.

Eugene. (much later). Can we identify pupils for a structured setting? (Tome cites a case in which two students are holding up fourteen).

Eugene. How many are like this?

Tom. About 20 percent . . . They haven't had the training. May be we should back up and give it to them.

Alec. Some need one teacher. They are not ready.

Eugene. We've said pupils are responsible. We might have to reverse it.

Tom. It doesn't have to be all years, David.

Alec. One teacher and some of us coming in would be a big step for some.

Eugene. I asked Irma privately if she'd willing to take it. She said, 'Yes.'

Thus, in response to the number of students who were unable to schedule instruction, engaged in independent study, and move in the program, at the close of Day 2 the ISD team decided on a self-contained room.

It was decided that the identification of pupils for the self-contained group would begin the following day. Irma's group was to have access to the math resource person 40 minutes daily and the science resource person three days week.

These skill difficulties were not the only problems experienced by some of the students. The planning and coordination of instructional periods, Training Groups, and other students activities were dealt with in a number of lengthy staff team meetings. There were no precedents with which to compare and to contrast the current attempt. Staff coordination problems were pronounced. Although the following segment indicates early considerations on the implementation of student scheduling, it also points to the lack of clarity concerning procedural matters.

Liz. If you have a 45 minutes period..

Alec. How can you have a 45-minute period?

Liz. Well, if you let them schedule their own.

Irma. What about the group plan? Are we going to let them stay in groups?

Alec. Yes, but they may work independently.

(Observer: David points out that they may not be able to keep permanent groups, since they are not "flexible" — more security at first— permanent groups—can form subgroups).

David. It is going to require skills in scheduling. . . I hadn't realized it is essential to the whole thing. . . should we schedule the first week and go from there.?

(*Observer:* Liz doesn't know exactly how much time she needs. Kay wants 30 minutes time periods at first. David wants schedule so that period can vary from 15 minutes to an hour; an time schedule sheet to schedule groups for 15 minutes to an hour).

As a consequence of the difficulties, individual scheduling replaced group "singing up" in an attempt to keep closer check on pupil activity. In the course of this, David defended group scheduling on the basis of its social aspects and on its enabling students to learn to work in groups. Others believed that the groups would form naturally and favored letting social groups come as they would. David, on the other hand, continued to maintain that children should leave groups only by mutual consent with pupil groupings and that they should learn how to cope. His view was opposed by Shelby, Tom, Alec and Irma.

The decision to change the scheduling was announced to the students to be effected the following week. In reply to a student's question about the problem of pupils erasing others' names from schedule sheets, Alec replied: "This freedom we don't have. We can't erase names. I hope it doesn't happen again. We don't want to have to tell you everything you do. . . For that reason don't erase them. If the group is filled up, tell the instructor."

The early difficulties of the students, in part, highlight the absence of clearly defined decision-making areas for the faculty. At least two of the faculty and principal were unsure as to what their roles were. At the second day's meeting, Mr. Shelby spoke of the lack of clarity in his role. He cited it as a "personal problem" and that he did not know "whether to lead, be a resource person, or just a member of the group." "The materials specialist also pointed out several times that he recognized things that needed attention, but he did not know whether or not they were in his area of jurisdiction. A part of this lack of clarity seems to have grown from the initial assumption that the faculty structure would entail no hierarchy but, instead, all would have equivalent opportunities for decision-making and action. The role of Walt Larsen, Kirkham's replacement, also was undefined. The impact of the ambiguity of the situation became more pronounced as the reorganization in ISD was attempted.

By the time of the second reorganization, there had been two major deviations from the initial plan with respect to allocation and organization of the faculty. The first involved David, who originally was to have been a full-time academic counselor, and who became the director of the student Training Groups. As in indicated elsewhere, faculty sentiments towards the continuation and value of the Training Group sessions varied. When Irma, who with David was to have been the other academic counselor, was assigned a self-contained group, the organizational structure was further changed. The consequences of these two deviations from the original plan were not clearly foreseen.

The third structure. During a lengthy team meeting (until 7:30 p.m.) decisions were made that further altered the organization of both the faculty and the students. Each of the resource people was to have designated teaching station at which he worked consistently; during the course of a day was to meet 40 to 45 students in each of four sessions in his subject matter area. In addition to this, he was to spend time with Irma's pupils in the self-contained group. Another changed centered on John, the physical education resource person at this time he was freed to assume his duties as a full-time resource person in physical education. The children were to be in a six-block schedule: language arts, science, mathematics, social studies, physical education, and Training Groups. David,s totao schedule was student Training groups: these left him free in the afternoon. As a contrast, both the math and the physical education resource persons were having difficulties finding the free time to eat lunch and to spend time with the self-contained group, which was taking their free period.

The above changes were essentially a shift to large group instruction, which the program initially had sought to avoid. The modification was made at Principal Shelby's suggestion, which , in turn, was made in part in response to parental reaction. The faculty members, however, viewed the changes as being effected primarily under Shelby's inpetus. As the statements below indicate, teacher sentiments with respect to the instructional changes were varied as of September 14.

Tom. We've lost a battle but not the war. I fear the school would have blown up. I see it as necessary if the school is going to continue.

(Observer: At this point the development of the team, Tom seemed to fill an unofficial role of coordinator and acting principal).

Kay. I'm quite opposed. I don't like the large group instruction, and it doesn't fit what I want to do?

Jack. I'm in agreement. This is more what I wanted anyway, I can't see how you can run a program and other way:

Liz. I'm unhappy that I don't have materials with which to work.

Alec. I see it as a necessary setback. I will have some of the my groups on independent project immediately.

John. I'm pleased to be back in physical education. Someone else suggested it, but I am in agreement.

David was in agreement with those who viewed large group instruction as a necessity at that point. At the time, he was still engaged as T-group trainer, was happy with the position, and regarded it as essential. Some days later other staff members expressed the feeling that David's Training Groups gave him a lighter load than they, and they subsequently voted to discontinue the groups.

Walt Larsen was not present at the meetings. Shelby had told Walt that he did not have to attend team meetings in that he might be at Kensington four days or four weeks. The consequences of the failure to make an attempt to integrate Walt into the ISD team were pronounced. His ill-defined role has already been mentioned, yet he was criticized by many of the faculty for assuming a definite stance in the organization. Presumably he might have been a valuable asset in the weeks following the reorganisation when, in effect, both academic counsellors directed their energies elsewhere to Training Groups and to the self-contained room. However, he had no directive or job definition within which to operate.

Statements cannot be as to what his effectiveness might have been had his position been clarified; however, the fact remains that few attempts were made to "build him to the faculty" and, if anything, were discouraged. He, in turn, showed little or no initiative. This seems a significant issue in staff utilization at a time when extra personnel were needed. These events also had the effect of perpetuating misgivings about the dismissal of Kirkham.

Summary: The Continuous Coping with unanticipated Consequences.

At one point in our data analysis we thought of subtitling the book, "organizational change, the continuous coping with latent and unanticipated consequences." The thesis we perceived was that each resolution of a tremendously difficult and complex problem created a host of consequences, new problems which, at best, had only been partially foreseen. ISD's third structure was soon to give way with the dissolution of the self-contained class and the elimination of the Training groups. Rumours were life concerning the removal of some of the ISD staff and also the replacement of ISD staff with one or more of the Basic Skills staff. Neither of these events came to pass. However, the dissatisfaction with the instructional program and the continued serious interpersonal staff conflict and hostility led, on November 3, to another major reorganization of ISD into two teams. The gym was split into the North and the South. This separation was accompanied by the physical closing of high gymnasium room divider and seemed of great importance. Later, further changes occurred as the North team split once again into a self-contained classroom and team of two. The program in both sides of ISD included some "teaming" in the sense of joint planning and some departmentalization, although most of the instruction occurred in the context of the self-contained classroom.

The consequences varied from mundane to major. All seemed to pose special problems. Selections from the field notes illustrate them.

One of the more striking aspects of the team meeting of ISD centered on the impact of the split into two teams on minor events. Such as the availability of tempra paints, and whether they should be store in central unit, and whether there would be any left if they were stored in a central unit. This kept raising the "fair share" type of the issue. The unit about which people organize their thoughts is now a team of three rather than an individual of one or a team of six. Books, supplies, passageways, time for lunch, entrances and exits, and the like, all need to be reconsidered and settled (11/7).

Several of the more significant consequences were noted a short time later.

At the close of the day I had a chance to chat briefly with Liz, Kay and Alec, individually and together. The north side seems to have resolved its division into three relatively self-contained classrooms. This distresses Liz to a very great extent and Kay almost not at all. Kay foresees a shift coming shortly as they begin to move about for instructional purpose. As a language arts specialist, Liz, literally is not prepared to teach elementary in all the subject matter areas and just does not know what to do. She has little conception of how to organize and to set up a science program or to organize and to set up a math program, and so forth. She is a very interesting example of someone trained for a speciality, and then the speciality collapses. Now she must be an all-purpose kind of person and she does not have the skills or the knowledge to carry it out. Earlier, when the teams had been compared on experience, it wasn't experience so much that was critical but, instead, the lack of training on the part of some, especially Liz. Added to this is the fact that David has very strong preferences not to instruct at all; these two in combination give the team its unhappy flavor. They do have an important foothold on the discipline problem, which they may or may not realize. The classes were much more orderly on the North side than I've ever seen them. This is especially true of Liz's group. Now would seem to be an optimal time for her to strike and develop "challenging" lessons. She apparently does not have the resources to do it; the school the team, and Eugene are not there to provide it. Some very simple instructional help in a repetitive style of traditional teaching could get the instructional program off the ground (11/11).

The observers hypothesized further regarding the conceptual issues involved in the organizational change. Initially, the researchers phrased the problem as the impact of the internal system back on the external system. Or, in other terms, the impact of the informal organization on the formal structure or formal organization.

With almost no consideration to the explicit problems of the learning objectives for pupils, and of the means of reaching them, the reorganization was brought about because various team members had considerable difficulty working with each other. We should point out also that there was some concern about the departmentalization and the fact that this was a far cry from the team set-up that most of team had desired initially. It redid the formal structure in the sense of eliminating academic counselors and making everyone an instructor. It shifted the movement of the students through the school day to a very different pattern. Specialization is retained with physical education but with practically no one else. Until things settle down to some extent, they will approach their teaching in this self-contained fashion. There are consequences in terms of the way kids go to lunch and with whom they eat. There are also consequences with regard to which students are working together. A variety of aspects of friendship structure patterns have been broken up. Several kids have commented within earshot of the observers that they wish they were with their friends or could they switch and be with their friends. Some of this is within North and South, and some of it is between North and South. Some of the same old language arts difficulties on the South Side recur with Jack and Alec, especially when Jack has to teach some of these things. Although the South Side three may have an easy and friendly social and ideological compatibility, they may get hung up also on the specialization skills that do not fit the current situation.

The interplay in other schools and situation between the domination of the textbooks for (1) a vehicle that puts you through areas that you do not know well, and (2) as an easy set of program decisions that then saves you time for other things, or just saves you time in terms of the heavy wear and tear of teaching, seems more and more cogent. Part of the parameters of this seem to be how many things can one be creative about and excited about at one time. Is it better to do a major exciting, innovative job in language arts and social studies and give a kind of ride in science and math, or in another two areas, or one or three, rather than in six or seven? This seems particularly true for a new teacher who has, I guess, a number of things to learn (11/11).

Thus, the third reorganization involved major changes in the organization of the faculty, resulting in essentially two teams of three. This division left the teams unbalanced in terms of faculty specialization and preparation. For example, the North team had no one highly skilled in math and science; the difficulties arising form this lack of specialization were coupled with the absence of standard textbooks. Problems of the allocation and storage of materials and supplies also increased. The erection of a wall between the two teams enhanced the difficulties relating to pupil movement. Access to lunch, rest rooms, and library facilities for students on the South was gained only by going through the full length of the North team area. Also the supervision of pupils became more difficult, since instead of all sharing responsibility in some way for the entire group, after the division, students could be designated as "ours" and "theirs." Thus, the third reorganization had far-reaching implications for spatial, interpersonal, and organizational variables. The systemic quality of the issues ranging from the alteration of the formal doctrine to role specialization of faculty is readily apparent.

Subsequent to the North-South division (split), the North team of three divided leaving a team of two and one self-contained room. The latter division had its source primarily in differences of belief about the degree of structure the instructional program should have. Two of the team members wanted a designated time for instruction in specific subject matter areas, but one wanted students to be permitted to schedule activities independently at any time. After being unable to reach a compromise on procedure, they decided on the two-one split. The ramification of this decision are indicated in a later chapter.

Transition Division

The Transition Division had a team of three teachers and approximately 90 students. In temporary quarter they were provided with the one large room and two additional classrooms. The summary notes indicate some of the primary concerns of the team in the first few days of the early part of the year.

The Transition teachers indicated at the end of the first day that nothing had gone right. The buses did not come until almost 5:00 p.m., which made it a very long workday because some of the students started arriving before 9:00 a.m., that morning.

The principal came by from ISD and said: “Don't ask how things went. Things can go no way except getting better; the situation is certainly no hopeless.”

Both Meg and Claire agreed that possibly the next day they would use more traditional methods. The next day one of the team remarked, “today we rule the students; whereas, yesterday they ruled.”

Meg feels that not enough transfer exists between the work that goes on in the smaller groups and that which takes place in the group of 90. Yesterday, for one hour and a half, 60 of the students remained in one room while the others went out for reading courses. Meg and Claire feel that this (the activity of the 60) was busy work and waste of time; however, Dan feels that it was not wasted, that it was good experience for the students.

Claire mentioned that they may go toward the more traditional, at least, for a while. It seems that both she and Meg will move in that direction. It is difficult to locate quite where Dan is standing or really just what he wants to do. he seems to disagree with some of the thing that they have been saying, especially concerning what they saw as work and the more traditional methods; however, thus far he has offered few alternatives from which to choose.

Claire feels that the students are never busy. Meg describes the noise as "chaos" and she feels that most of it is their fault, i.e., the fault of the teachers, because they are not quite sure what they are trying to do and they have not been able to facilitate the activities that they have initiated. Another remarks that she feels stupid when she stands before a group and talks and yet knows that no one hears because they are talking so loud themselves. She says that the activities have not been fitted to the children, and part of this is because they haven't really got to know the children. Their failure to know the children is attributed to groups that are too large and of inconsistent membership. She observed that the children for not know how to use time and that they are tired of not doing anything. They also feel that there is not enough carry over and new activity.

Meg and Claire want to break into smaller groups; however, Dan hold out for the larger group for a while. He thinks that there are certain tasks that can combat what has been causing the trouble in the larger groups. When asked about specific tasks, he suggests some kind of ditto materials possibly taken form second grade workbooks because they are not quite sure yet where the children are reading or at what level they are doing other work.

Claire pointed out that thus far there are not any library books. However, Dan went to find out that they will be able to use the library on Monday.

They discussed the reading activity that was held in the afternoon, and they finally concluded that things were so noisy that it really was not a fair test of the students' reading levels. Meg thinks that the teachers must know at what level students are reading before they try to prepare any seat work activities that are of any value other than providing busy work. Claie noted that students' shifting back and forth between teachers makes for difficulty in coordinating assignments.

Some discussion centered on the arrangement of desks and chairs and the allocation of space in the large room. Meg pointed out that one reason why they are not functioning any better than they are at the present time is because they have kids, as she says, "wall to wall" and that there are no interest centers as such; everyone is just thrown together.

This led to a further consideration of pupil groups and organization. At the close of a lengthy meeting,they decided to assign thirty students each team member. At the same time, each noted that this division of the students is contrary to the Kensington philosophy, which none of them is sure will work (9/10).

Thus the primary concerns of the Transition Division centered about the size and structure of pupil group, the assessment of student skills, the types of activity, the allocation of space, and the coordination of teacher effort. However, the shortage of materials, few library books, and few textbook were also reflected in the instructional program that developed. But overshadowing the early days of the Transition Program were numerous comments made by the faculty who measured their present classroom practices with what they had interpreted as the doctrine of an individualized educational program.

Basic Skills Division

Early in the second week of the summer workshop, Basic Skills had split into a team of two and team of four. The reasons lay generally in staff disagreement and conflict concerning significance of teaching experience, the importance and legitimacy of basal readers in an individualized program, and several personal issues. As we have indicated, the work of the two teams was carried out independently.

Basic Skills: Team 4

The field notes at noon on the first day indicated that the team of four had an array of major an minor problems.

I just spoke briefly to one of the teachers about her conception of the next few days or weeks. She said that she hopes that they will be split into reading groups very shortly because she is all set and ready to go. She felt that the others in the subgroups of four were not yet ready to divide, but she feels there is no other way to proceed. She stated that she had suggested several times that they divide into reading grounds either vertically or horizontally and that they begin the work of teaching an individualized reading program. She felt that the group had not picked up her cues and said that she could only wait and hope that they would do so soon. It appears that the team will be forced into a division of this kind quite shortly. They were very much confused today and had a difficult time in holding the children's interest for a long period of time. Compounding their problems are physical surroundings which are at best inconvenient. The lunch procedure promises to be one of the major difficulties. The time was switched about six times as Jean put it, and right now she did not know when it would be. When I left at 1:10 p.m., the first child had not yet entered. They had planned to get in as early as 12:30 or 12:40 (9/8).

Midweek. Notes from the middle of the week indicate that the Basic Skills Division was rapidly becoming aware of the nuances of team teaching.

The subgroup 4 seemingly gained more insight to facilitate the teaching of reading. They were to end their period at 10:45 At 10:45 the entire Team-4 had planned to go outside for P.E. activities. Sue came to Wanda, Jean, and Elaine and told them that their activities with the second grade were so helpful and beneficial that they did not wish to break at this time. They wanted to keep their group a while longer. Neither of the tree teachers wished to oppose do with the schedule that had been previously agreed on by the team at last night's meeting. Wanda said, "I'll take all 70 of the first graders outside for P.E." This left Elaine and Jean free to take a break. I spoke to them for 10 or 15 minutes about the problems attendant to this kind of spur-of-the-moment decision-making. In this discussion both Jean and Elaine saw very clearly the problems that this brings about. Jean mentioned that this *lack* of structure bound her a great deal. I asked for further clarity. She said, in something close to this fashion, "In my own self-contained classroom, I had all the freedom in the world. I could extend a learning experience, or shorten it, or cut it completely if I wished. Here, I'm forced into a rigid schedule." She said that it seems very odd and yet the freedom that they wanted was the things that inhibited them and made them more rigid. Elaine agreed that 25 children and self-contained classroom would be far superior for the very objectives that they wish to achieve. They both felt that decisions as the one Sue and Chris had made were sometimes beneficial to the group making the decision, but it certainly disrupted matters for the rest of the children. Elaine gave the example that perhaps a group of 15 children were involved in very meaningful learning experience and, therefore, the teacher of these 15 would simply arbitrarily state that the period would be extended for an extra 30 minutes. Although this may be fine for the group of 15, the group of 55 would have to find some makeshift busy work to kill time.

Last night, the Basic Skills group met after the day's sessions. All seemed very tired confused. The bus schedule was in a state of turmoil. The were ready for the children to leave at about 3:50 p.m., but had to wait until at least 4:30 or 4:40 before they actually cleared the building. After the children were gone the group met in subgroups of two and four. Chris met with the subgroup of four. After some informal discussion of how confused the day's activities were, Chris suggested that they were all rather "wilted" and that perhaps they had better meet in the morning. Wanda would have none of this. He said, "Absolutely not. I will not go home until I know what I'm going to do tomorrow. I will not go through another day like today." The main discussion centered on grouping or not grouping the children and what type of group of use. Wanda held out very firmly for the need for reading groups on ability levels. She suggested that they separate first graders from second graders and then group within each grade. Jean and Sue were not quite ready to break down into first and second grades. They seemed to want to hold on to a more novel approach to education but do not quite know how. Chris felt they could continue the present division for a few days at least until they had given the children a chance to settle down. Wanda was pushing very hard for a division in ability groupings for the next day. Elaine seemed sure that today had not worked well but did not quite know how best to proceed. Some of the discussion centered on whether the children should have assigned desks—Sue and Jean holding out for a freer home base. Wanda was not overly impresses with tradition at this point;

she just wanted to get some teaching done. The group finally decided to spend one hour in this morning session divided into first and second grades for a language arts periods.

Chris and Sue will take the second grade group and have a large reading group. They will be doing free reading with some of discussion of the material. Elaine Jean and Wanda will take the first graders in random selection and attempt to evaluate their readiness or reading level. I feel pretty sure that Wanda will continue to push for ability groupings even within the grade level; however, it will take a little more time to evaluate the children and to divide them in this manner. They are still holding on to their random groupings across grades (9/9).

Later notes indicate that there were some continuing problems with grouping. Also great effort was made to avoid the fate of a self-contained classroom.

Some summary thoughts concerning last night's Basic Skills team meeting. Jean appeared to give the most leadership in the last night's meeting. She threw out many of the big questions that needed to be discussed. It seemed that once issues were brought out, they were not followed to conclusion. This seems to stem, again in part, from everyone's inability to follow a point to conclusion for fear of not getting group consensus or some other such group process problem. The Basic Skills subgroup 4 seemed to stack up somewhat in this fashion. Wanda, Elaine, and jean, all three, seemed very dissatisfied with their own classroom work thus far. Elaine and Wanda seem to make statements in unison on several occasions that reflected their views of their own deficiencies up to this point. Wanda is quite convinced that it is because of the unworkability of the four-man team. She has tried to insert this on several occasions but received little support. Elaine also feels it is not working but does not seem quite as sure as Wanda that it cannot work.

Several statements were made to the effect that they had subscribed to this type of philosophy for several years and, in fact, were much more successful in the traditional self-contained classroom than they have been in attempting to implement this at Kensington. Sue seems to steer clear of any removal of the subgroup of four. She does not want to get tied to a two-man team. She seemed to dread even more the thought of a self-contained classroom. Jean's position is a striving for some workable plan for their group that would not mean self-contained classrooms and also would not mean departmentalization. She wants a little flexibility in that she could utilize the strength of another teacher; however, she deplores the rigidity of attempting to conform to a fixed time schedule. Jean seems to have the right the questions, but seemingly no one has the right answers. Chris is quite content with the way things are going and, in fact, said that they had made a lot of progress and that she would like to work out a few of the bugs in the program but, in general, she thought that sings had gone quite well.

Wanda appeared quite concerned with the general behavior of the children. She stated last night that they were wilder than any children she had ever seen. In part, the wants to have more control of the children in their walking from classroom to classroom, is going to the lunchroom, to the bathroom, and the like. Sue expressed her interest in having no part of this arrangement. She said that the children will simply learn, and very soon, that they will want to walk from one class to another. Wanda is still most concerned about the image of teacher as controller and, as such, wishes a great deal more structure. Chris mentioned that the Basic Skills 2 had a much smoother operation. She noted that the teachers led the children from class to class and had the children sitting down quietly before they left them. She didn't seem to place any value judgment on this (9/15).

Thus, in addition to the limited temporary physical facilities and the coordination of their schedules with the ones of the high school in which they were temporarily located, Basic Skills-4 were not without their differences with respect to ideas about student grouping, teaching method, and choice of subject matter. As is indicated in the notes, the form that teacher-pupil organization would take was not delineated in detail at the outset of the Basic Skills-4 program. Varying sentiments were expressed about possible alternatives; they ranged from defending the self-contained classroom to advocating the elimination of fixed time schedules, which are viewed as rigid and inflexible. Also the self-evaluations of their performance as a team were just as disparate; some indicated approval of the program, but others felt that much improvement, if not revamping, was needed.

Basic Skills: Team 2

On September 7, the day before the pupils arrived, the research staff summarized and interpreted their views of Basic Skills Team-2.

Subteam 2 seems to be working quite smoothly on the surface. Carla is a strong teacher, having taught 27 years in the elementary and, especially, in the primary field. She has never had a year off from teaching since she began as a two-year graduate 27 years ago. This lengthy experience has given her the feeling, and perhaps rightfully so, that she has experienced about every aspect of teacher-pupil behaviour that is possible. She is quite firm and set in her ways and makes most of the decisions for the subgroup.

Mary at times seems quite firm and able to make up her own mind and yet, at other times, seems quite willing to go along with Carla. Both have little patience for the so-called "discussion or process" method of the workshop. Both feel that the larger team meetings are a waste of time and both feel that much more can be done by working in small groups. I feel that this subgroup of two will have little contact with the other subteam of four in the Basic Skills Division. It will be interesting if the group that supposedly is departing the farthest from the Institutional Plan will perhaps work the smoothest and most efficiently. It will depend a great deal on how busy Eugene is with the other phases of the school program, especially the Independent Study Division, whether or not he will have time to supervise the Basic Skills. I am sure that he would not be pleased without the fact that they will be conducting what very well could be a double self-contained classroom atmosphere. I also feel that this subgroup of two will have a very definite plan in mind by the time the entire school gets into the new Kensington building. It will be very difficult at this time to revamp and to reorganize the Basic Skills into any other division, than it now has, namely, a subgroup of four and a subgroup of two.

This group will house all the pupils in their section in one of the classrooms having 60 desks in one room. They will then use the second room that is assigned to them for small group activity, such as reading groups, creative art, music, and the like. It would appear that these two teachers will work rather effectively together, introducing a good "traditional" atmosphere for the children (9/7).

I effect, the predictions were borne out. Number work began in the first days and beginning work in set theory of the new math was not far behind. The basal reading materials, On Your Way, were distributed and in use very quickly also. The program was academic oriented but traditional.

Later conversations solidified the coherence of predictions, teaching style and points of view.

Yesterday after sessions on Thursday I spent some time talking to Carla and Mary. Both of them feel that the rest of the Basic Skills plus Transition and Independent Study seem to be going in a direction of which they do not approve. It seems that neither of these two teachers would strongly support the Kensington philosophy if confronted by one of the patrons. Mary had compared the vagueness of Kensington with the solidity of her own child in the Jefferson School. She stated that he had come home with a sheet which very clearly outlined the goals and the expectations that they hope to achieve. By contrast she felt Kensington had not done this in any way. I attempted to remain neutral by stating that I did not know which of the two I would prefer. Evidently they read my statement to be a criticism of Kensington's vagueness and both laughed out loud at this comment. Carla considers herself a middle-of-the-roader and stated that she has been the same type of person in her self-contained classroom for the last 10 years or so.

I feel that both Carla and Mary's having taught fourth grade last year poses certain real problems for their adjustment to the first grade. Mary stated that she was very tired and tense working with the little folks. She said that she did not realize that so much lead up was necessary. She stated, "They cannot even write their own name and I even had to teach them how to use a jump-rope outside." She commented that she wishes she had stayed in the Transition Division as she had previously wanted to (9/11).

Thus, subteam 2 developed independently of the rest of the Basic Skills Division and, in effect, apart from the total school both in terms of actual classroom behavior and ideology. Communication between the subteams was quite limited, and Eugene focused little attention on the subteam. Later the split into two subteams came to be rationalized as a facet of the doctrine, with team 3 described as an expanded self-contained classroom. For whatever reasons, it was a characteristic of Kensington and its doctrine that such wide variation in structure and method were permitted.

Some Early Interpretations

Although the field notes contain a wealth of further detail on the fall day-to-day events of Kensington, it seems more feasible at this point to say a few general things that later will be considered in the more detailed analysis.

From the beginning, as is pointed out in earlier description of the three temporary physical plants, study and instruction were somewhat altered and structured by the makeshift facilities. A significant amount of materials and equipment had not arrived by the opening of school. This deficit was especially critical at Kensington where textbooks and "traditional" teacher helps were discouraged which, in turn, placed even greater emphasis on para-instructional supplies, increased the pressure on, the materials specialists, and heightened faculty tension in the face of a shortage of materials. The latter was especially important, since the faculty was to serve as the means to create the majority of the learning tasks to be used with pupils.

Attempts at coordination of bus times with the existing district schools resulted in uncertainties, long waits, and growing parental disapproval. With no formally agreed-on procedure whereby students were to be dismissed, the variability of the schedule emphasized internal problems in the ISD. With 200 Children in one room, this lack of uniformity increased faculty tensions. Coupled with this was the fact that once decisions were made, members failed to adhere to them, and in other instances all were not informed as to the action to take. As becomes clearer elsewhere in this book, often when there was ample access to and knowledge about facilities and materials, deficiencies in the structure precluded their satisfactory use.

Another factor that required adjustment on the part of both faculty and students was the noise level. It was high in all of the divisions, and the staff was unable to speak loudly enough to be heard by all of the children. Initially, in the Basic Skills Division, teachers had to do the reading instead of the students. The minimized opportunities for pupil oral reading. In the Transition Division three whistles were in evidence, and in the ISD Liz, among others, was losing her voice and she "couldn't hear herself." Even though he expected it to be a problem, Tom noted that, "the noise level was a good bit higher than he had anticipated." In a later section we consider more fully issues such as "openness to extraneous stimuli."

Combined with the difficulties in quelling the noise was the sheer number of children that each staff member under the initial organizational plan was required to contact and to come to know. Learning the names of 200 children and something about each, as would be expected from the "usual" elementary teacher, seemed an insurmountable task at Kensington.

An early and continuing problem was that the majority of children were unable to devise and to carry out individual plans of work. Their being capable of doing this was crucial to the success of "individualized" study—an integral part of the Kensington program. This deficit, along with a lack of materials and limited teacher time and preparation, took an early toll and, in turn, was an incentive for the poor use of pupil time that both parents and some faculty came to view as a "waste." In addition, the children lacked adequate skills to work together in groups, which was another necessary capability to function well at Kensington. The wandering and milling about in the gym continued and were accompanied by clay throwing, paper air planes, further misuse of materials (most usually confined to individual tables), and a general restlessness.

Time demands of the program also were increasingly great. Since this is discussed in other parts of the book, a brief mention is sufficient here. Team, subteam, and planning meetings began to take several hours a week before or after school and in the evenings. The Transition Division, in part, was unable to find the time to plan enough activities for a large group and resolved the problem of dividing the students into three groups.

Another area that contributed to creating disillusionment was the repeated and continuing dilemma of reorganization. The sources of the reorganizations lay generally in some of the problems mentioned previously and in parental reaction. Conditions that preceded the various organizational modifications and their apparent "failure," in part, made for dissatisfaction and a lowering of morale. The frequent reorganizations emphasized movement from specialists to generalists among the staff. This was in conflict with the original positions they were given when hired.

We observed previously that many were selected for their specialities, skills, and training for secondary education. Yet a few weeks after school began, faculty members with at best two areas of competency were teaching a variety of subjects as would have been the case in a self-contained classroom. Other than its being an unfortunate use of manpower, this condition deviated from the original plan for the school and added to the growing faculty disappointment and consequent morale problems.

By October, much of the August and September enthusiasm was partially translated into disillusionment, either of a personal or a team nature. A number of internal and external facets of the organization were instrumental in altering the initial hope, Several in the ISD were very discouraged; two members of the Basic Skills team were thinking of quitting at mid-term. In addition to this, the notes indicate that "almost everybody is giving serious thought to not coming back next year" (10/23). As the introductory epilogue points out, this is in fact what did happen.

There were many reasons for the early despair. Some of the faculty were vocal and the basis of their grievances more easily observable. Kay is recorded as "very tired and discouraged." She's sick of the dust, dirt, the confusion, and the lack of order She's also tired of the noise. One teacher was asked whether or not she had talked with the principal. She replied, "No, not directly; it's his baby, and you can't tell a person that his baby is no good." She was also displeased with the departmentalized organization that the ISD had developed and "would just as soon have her own self-contained classroom."

David was also experiencing progressive disillusionment and disenchantment. He noted three primary areas of dissatisfaction: (1) the shift from process, (2) the loss of the student T-groups, and (3) the inability of the team to function as a group. His vehemence against formal instruction and his refusal to "teach" in the usual sense of the word was known by the faculty; however, our discussion clearly shows the strength of his feelings was put to the test by the third reorganization.

Eugene was also troubled. His discontent centered primarily on four areas, none of which were mutually exclusive: (1) the "sterile program" being offered in some of the classes, (2) his personal anxiety, (3) the deficiencies of the faculty, and (4) his relationship with one of the consultants. He saw the problems as crossing division lines but as stopping short of encompassing any one entire division. At this time he described his feelings as those of "general apprehension and anxiousness" (10/14). A week later he again noted that he was not "functioning very well" and "was not getting as much done as he had hoped to do." One specific items expresses some of his general feelings. In commenting about the interpretation and feedback of materials from the recordings on the consultant's research projects, Eugene indicated that they would probably have to be done by him. Although he was trained and competent to do this, when he has feeling tense and nervous this got communicated also, and the situation did not go so well.

His feelings about the inadequacies of the staff were also still much in evidence. He specifically mentioned one teacher and her inability as an instructor or leader. Later he was considering her release. What seems to be of importance is that little attempt was made to help the faltering team members. In fact, the several organizations placed some staff members at an even greater disadvantage.

Eugene's discontent with Roberts, the consultant, began early in their relationship and continued until the relationship was terminated during the second semester. Eugene notes that their rapport was "not good" and that the conversations "flitted around from topic to topic, rather than seriously moving in and attacking basic issues." He reported that he confronted Roberts with questions of bad rapport, and that they "could never get anywhere because of that," and that he wanted to "talk about his feelings" in regard to this. He perceived Roberts as listening only briefly and then shifting the conversation to something else.

These then are some of the sources of early discouragement experienced by the staff. Following the thread of these early difficulties through the remaining months of school, to the demise of some and the resolution of others, indicates that one of the overshadowing issues was the departure of the school from the expectations stated in the doctrine. The notes confirm that most of the faculty expressed concern and, in some respects, disappointment over their failure to adhere most closely to the doctrine. The subsequent organizational development in light of these sentiments is described in later chapters.

The Move to the New Building

Introduction. On Wednesday, November 25, the staff bulletin contained this item:

"*Moving date*. Rapid progress is being made on the building, but there are still many things to be done before it will be ready for pupils. Although we may start moving some things in next week, it does not appear that the building will be ready for pupils until the following week. No definite date has been set, but we shall see."

The next bulletin, No. 24, the following Tuesday, carried the specifications:

"*Moving arrangements*. As of this moment (1:52 p.m.) plans have been made to move the office and the ISD into the new building on Thursday and Friday of this week. Cabinetry and equipment will be moved Thursday and Friday morning, and pupil desks and chairs will be moved Friday afternoon. ISD pupils will be dismissed at 1:00 p.m. Friday. They should be instructed to take all personal belongings and books, etc., home with them.

"The same arrangements will be followed for the BSD and TD the following week, December 10 and 11."

The bare announcements of the move convey little of the flesh and blood of the move itself. The children were engaged in busy work; the literal aches and pains of the staff were evident. The interplay of long-term and short-term commitments was visible also. The notes indicate the tenor of these events.

As I looked around the room the kids seemed to be engaged in a whole variety of busy-work type activities and holding actions. Some of them were working with SRA materials, some were watching ETV or folms and some of them were listlessly sitting. Others were playing magic-square type games. Liz had on the overhead projector a picture of the Kensington School and was, in effect, telling them about where they would be going and what they would do. John was still looking kind of depressed about the move. He's not going to teach his Transition PE class this afternoon so that he can come over and get his materials and equipment arranged. He also commented that Tom has sprained his back and has some difficulties."

Kay told me also that there was some discussion about whether the Saturday team meeting would be at the new building or whether it would be in the central offices as originally designated. She's eager to get over and begin work on the set-up for Monday. John also talked in that same vein. Kay did not have any idea what was going to be on the agenda of the staff meeting and it was her hope that it was not going to take all morning.

In Transition, Claire raised several times questions as to why the kids were not excused from school and time given to the move. Mrs. Beacon commented that the most desirable time would be on Monday. She just does not see how they are going to be ready for the kids then.

It's now 3:00 p.m., and I'm leaving the new building for the day. David just came over a few minutes ago, and Liz and Kay came by for a few minutes more recently. I caught part of a brief discussion among Liz, Kay, Tom and Irma. The topic centered on the problem of the instructional areas, and, initially, whether there would be chairs and tables there. Tom said "eventually" but he didn't know whether they'd be ready by Monday. Liz, with a very strained and nervous laugh, commented that she was interested in eventually but was concerned about Monday. This led into a discussion of the utilization of the areas. Irma suggested that she and Aleck and Jack had talked about the possibility of having one area belong to one team and the other area belong to the other team and share the third space—on a sign-up basis. There are some potential problems in this because the Transition Division apparently is to have access to those extra spaces also. One obvious solution would be for each of the teams to have one additional space. This will have some disadvantages in that the North teams has two subteams—David versus Kay and Liz—and Transition has in reality two subteams—Dan versus Meg and Claire.

Eugene had a telephone conversation with the principal of an adjacent school. He was discussing the custodian, which they shared, and whether it would be possible to have him come over to Kensington tomorrow morning to help arrange furniture.

The teachers are scrubbing out cabinets. Irma has a bucket of soapy water and is working on them. David has been working with a screwdriver and a pair of pliers trying to get the shelving back in shape in the cabinets. During the loading and unloading of materials and furniture everything had been piled over in the centre of the ISD area in the new building and the teachers were not free to have one person on the sending end and one on the receiving end to allocate what goes where and to whom things belong. Consequently the men, when they brought it, could not put it where it belonged; instead, they just let it plop into one big pile. Similarly, people are doing things such as cleaning cabinets and repairing shelves when the basic job seemingly ought to be to get the furniture moved into some kind of rough, approximate area, and the details can be cleaned up later or on another day. They will not be at all ready for the children's furniture when it arrives in the next 30 minutes or so. John is having difficulty finding space. When I saw him later, he had kind of a slap-happy mood about him and was looking over the basement room, which was full of paint buckets, a saw, and some other equipment and was a long cry from being cleaned up. It would be my guess that two men could not clean the thing out in the next two hours this afternoon.

Another item concerns David's asking the kids to volunteer, if they wished, to help tomorrow afternoon. He said about twelve were going to be coming in. He was concerned about what their parents would think of their coming in to help fix up the school. My reaction to him was that the parents would not mind at all if the kids wanted to. The point I didn't raise, and the one that seems most significant, will be the attitudes of the other teachers. My guess is that some will be unhappy just having the kids around and that others will be envious in that they did not get any kids to come in and help them.

Apropos of the whole organizational structure, and the affect toward it, it's appropriate to observe that neither of the student teachers, I guess, nor the permanent substitute showed up to help. On the one hand, you would think that they would want to and, on the other hand, one would think that they ought to. Perhaps the basic truth of it is the reflection on the satisfactions and the cohesion of the team, or the lack thereof (12/4).

Staff Reservations. Although the staff reactions to the move had a general cast of frustration and apprehension, there were individual nuances. For instance, one teacher commented to the observer:

She expressed a personal and private opinion which she had not talked about to the rest of the staff concerning what she calls respect for property. This arisen when I made a comment about how pretty the building was and she returned that she felt unhappy about letting the kids in the building for fear of what they will do to it. She considers respect for property as one of the fundamental aspects of our society and the views these kids as not having it. Interpretively, to me, what she's saying suggests that important impact of the nature of the freedom that they have given the children and how this has led to a misuse and wasting of materials and resources and to the lack of concern about the "nice things" that they have in the school. This point should be made in conjunction with one that is in the notes earlier somewhere about how different I saw these kids as compared to the downtown kids at the beginning of the year, especially in regard to their hostility and to their destructive behaviour, which I saw here as much less (12/4).

The overall reaction of the ISD staff was stated this way in the notes late on Friday afternoon.

The contrast in the sentiments of the professional staff to the sentiments of the non-professional staff, Mrs. Beacon, Arthur, and Inez, is one of a kind of grouchy gloominess versus childish excitedness in the latter. It ought to be a very happy occasion and, instead, it is very painful one, and this seems a very real tragedy (12/4).

The children's reactions. The notes during the afternoon of the first day, Monday, December 7, indicate the children's response to the new quarters.

In summary, all in all it seemed as if the move went very smoothly. The basic reaction I have about the children and their reactions to the building is one of high excitement and high positive affect toward the building. The building looks-new, it feels new, it smells new. It is difficult for me to take out my own excitement and parcel it out from the reactions of the children. As I watched them, they were eager to have a tour of the building, they were eager to see the different parts, they explored around, they wanted to know all about it. The carpets were well received in that the children kicked off their shoes and walked around in their stocking feet a good bit of the time (12/7).

Continuities in program and teacher style occurred as well in conjunction with new physical quarters.

Only a minimal amount of academic work occurred in the South Side group. Jack had on the board, as I felt, an assignment for a theme on their first day at school. At lunch he had commented that they had done a little oral reading. The lunch hour went amazingly well from my point of view. I had expected considerable confusion over this. The children were allowed to go to lunch a little before noon, shortly after the lines were set up, and they tended to go by class and by small numbers within classes. There seemed to be no difficulty with this at all. Mostly, they ate back in their classrooms under the supervision of their teachers, although there was some flexibility in this, since Linda, one of the student teachers, ate with Irma's group while Irma ate up in the curriculum lab. There were no long lines nor jam ups at the tables. They are eating 45 minutes to an hour before they did at the other building, which will make a very, very long afternoon. David's group already is behaving as they have in the other building, and they have been relatively unruffled by the change. His mode of operation looks a good bit like what Gouldner was calling the indulgency pattern in the gypsum plant. As I watched them this morning, there were one or two, especially a boy named George, when spent a good bit of time watching educational television, which David had running almost continuously. Another couple or several children were painting and doing art activities. Another one or two were working on SRA materials and a few more were wandering here and there and a few were working with cycloteachers. It's going to take a very careful and quantitative check and count to find out the number of kids who were engaging in academic-type activities and were busy this way as opposed to those who are just spending time. Liz's bunch remains the noisiest and the most "out of control" of the children (12/7).

In short, the two groups just mentioned were examples of the variation in pupil behavior that existed at Kensington. Overtly this aspect of the social structure changed little with the move to the new building.

The arrival of basic skills and transition. On Monday, December 14, the total staff and all the children were in the new building. In general, it was an exciting time for these pupils and the staff as well.

The day began surprisingly well. The children in Basic Skills and Transition were very excited and were pleased to be in the new school. This seemed to be reflected in the things that they did, the excitement with which they walked around, the questions they asked about the building, and the efficacy of the implied threats that "if you are not quiet, you won't be able to walk with us," which several of the staff used. There was a consistent lack of traffic in the perception core except right up to the end. Just before I left, the Basic Skills kids were out there with Chris and were looking for library books. I took a trip through ISD before I left, really before I had my last cup of coffee, and the view suggested that most of the people were pushing hard toward instructional programming (12/14).

On the following day, the flavor is maintained:

Lunch was kind of fun in that people kept adding to and leaving the group as they had free time. It started out with Liz alone, then Meg and I arrived; shortly thereafter Liz left and she was replaced by Claire and later Jean and Wanda and Kay, and then alternately David, Linda and Pat joined. Jean thought today was going better than yesterday because yesterday she was still suffering from a long and fatiguing weekend. Her patience ran out on her yesterday afternoon, she said. Wanda sees today as not better than yesterday because the kids have lost their focus and nobody seems to know where they are going or what they are doing. Much joking back and forth; for instance, when Wanda, Sue and Jean were planning and arranging schedules for this afternoon, Claire made a comment very close to "last minute planning, huh?" Wanda talked about all the problems with the red tape and the rules in terms of trying to get things done. If she can't find a wastepaper basket and some other things, she's going to "steal" one. Meg was furious with one of the aides who would hardly budge in terms of doing some work for her. As she put it to Jean, she cannot understand how the Basic Skills staff could have lived with her for 3 or 4 months as they have at Basic Skills. She said she never would have gotten anything if Tom had not come by. There was additional good humor as Dan came by wondering if Meg had seen his lunch. She told him where it was. Later she told the rest of us that she spent 5 to 10 minutes this morning going around from child to child trying to find out whose lunch this bag was. Later Dan indicated that the kids were teasing that Terrifico had eaten it. Sue was by, scrounging lunch off of several of the people, since she is on a diet and does not want to eat, yet she's hungry.

Wanda showed us how to cut out and make an elephant out of candycane and paper. It was quite novel and quite tricky. She learned this at a local nursery school. During this same interlude Meg commented that she had a number of different kinds of patterns and that the others in Basic skills were quite welcome to borrow them. This kind of trading seems to be an important part of the school. It extends the notion of the increased repertory as part of the experienced teacher personality. If they could once get things organized, this sharing of ideas could increase at a great rate and be most helpful to the newer teachers and to those with less skills in several areas (12/5).

The issues surrounding both formal and informal helping relationships are a part of the later analysis. Time limitations for materials construction by the staff, even with frequent exchanges in some of the teams were, as the later discussion indicates, quite severe.

The detached perspective: a summary. Methodologically, we instituted, by chance as we recall, an interesting procedure. From time to time, a research assistant who had been involved intimately in the first weeks of the summer workshop returned to see old friends and to observe the developments of the school. Although we did not realize it at the time, this provided a different kind of data. Although our major efforts were on the minutiae of social psychological analysis, we obtained a view of the proverbial forest instead of the trees. Illustratively, the notes contained these comments during the first week of the move into the new building.

My quick conversation with Paul centered on his feeling, (1) that they had no program yet, and (2) that their spirit was broken. Both of these points seem to me to be well taken. He commented also on sitting in on a discussion of religion with some of the kids, and the teacher was raising kinds of questions about who created God, and the like, which Paul saw as "risky" in the public schools. Several of the teachers apologized to him for what they were doing. In arithmetic they are going back to addition, subtraction, multiplication, and division in that they did not understand what had been occurring and they thought they would begin all over again. He commented that he sat in on one group while the teacher happened to be out of the room and the kids were wild and into all kinds of trouble. He commented also on the list of rules that apparently have staggered everybody in his eyes. As we stood outside and talked, the kids were going to and from lunch; some of them were in their slippers and some of them were in their stocking feet, and none of them had coasts on (12/10).

THE EXTENSION OF FORMALIZATION: SCHOOL RULES

Introductory Comments

The English language contains a number of words that reflect a common core of meaning: customs, mores, social norms, rules and laws. The essence of these terms refers to the expectations of members of a group, organization, or society that other members of the group will behave in certain ways. These expectations will vary in degree of formality; that is, social norms are commonly understood and rarely verbalized, but laws often are written and codified in considerable detail. Variations occur in the genesis of the understandings. In some instances they accumulate gradually both in acceptance and formality, as has common law. In some instances, the expectations as rules are established by fiat by a powerful individual or subgroup. The breadth of activities covered by the mores and laws varies considerably from group to group. Finally, the amount and kinds of surveillance, and the amount and kinds of rewards and punishments for conformity and deviation varies also.

In a formal organization, expectations in the form of rules function to facilitate goal attainment. In many instances, the rules are functional equivalents to orders or directives that have their genesis in goal attainment. This can introduce a variety of complexities when there are multiple and potentially conflicting goals, or when priorities among goals are not established. If goals are vague, ambiguous, or abstract, similar problems may arise. Furthermore, if the organization is to be democratically governed and administered, questions of who makes what decisions about which rules become critical also. Finally, the broader norms, meta norms, or "rules about rules" become a complicating context for any particular rule. For instance, Kensington's mandate and formal doctrine in accenting freedom and innovation minimized rules and traditions.

Changes at Kensington

Most school personnel, in their franker moments, will speak of rules and control of pupils as a necessity. In its simplest form, control means that pupils comply with school rules and the directives of teachers. The notes on December 9 indicates that problems of compliance of often unstated standards of conduct were occurring and, also, that the individual faculty members held varying standards.

Both of the men commented, on the way out, about the noise level that existed in the perception core. At that time, by a later count I made, there were about 60 kids working down there.

The kids were rather wild and much more like the first two weeks of school over at the junior high building. Part of this is because the several teachers are out today. Irma and Liz and ill, and Jack is at some kind of a meeting.

David's kids are roaming quite freely, and he lets them come and go as they please. One teacher told me that on Monday David's kids were wandering all over the building (12/9).